French Pl
Teacher's Book

GW00870532

Kate Corney
Moira Farrelly
Wendy Rydzkowski

Contents

Collins Educational
An imprint of HarperCollins*Publishers*

TARGET POPULATION

French Plus is designed for use by students following the National Curriculum programme of study at Key Stage 4 in French. It enables students, who would probably not achieve a GCSE grade G, to progress in suitable contexts, aligned with the National Curriculum programme of study.

The materials have specifically been written to complement the NEAB's Certificate of Achievement in French, but can be used with any students who may have difficulty in achieving a GCSE grade. They are associated with the language tasks in the NEAB Modern Foreign Languages syllabuses and these syllabuses complement the GCSE framework. The materials can, however, be used alongside any GCSE Modern Foreign Languages course.

USE OF THE TARGET LANGUAGE

Students are expected to understand instructions in the target language. Use of the target language is an element of good practice:

'Teachers should insist on the substantial use of the language for all aspects of the lesson.' (OFSTED)

There are times when this may not be appropriate. Students who suffer from a lack of confidence in foreign language learning will need particularly structured support, if lessons are to be conducted in the target language and you should not be afraid occasionally to use English, for example for explanations, and to establish discipline. Nevertheless, you should try to use the target language as much as possible. To help you, all instructions in the Student's Book, are in the target language, but care has been taken to limit these and to use cognates wherever possible. Rappel boxes appear on the pages of the Student's Book, offering a glossary of difficult vocabulary or phrases not met before.

On page 5, there is a list of all instructions used in **French Plus**. Students should be encouraged to refer to this when necessary. They should not, however, become totally dependent on this list and should aim gradually to need its support less and less.

When using instructions in the target language, try to support students' comprehension by some of the following methods:

- give clear examples of what you want
- use cognates wherever possible
- use mime and facial expression
- use visuals, if appropriate
- use another student to demonstrate the activity
- use a reliable volunteer as an interpreter

Never let students start an activity if the instructions have not been clearly understood. It is better to resort to English than to have a confused class.

Some useful classroom phrases

Regarde(z)	Look	Travaillez avec votre partenaire	Work with your partner
Ecoute(z)	Listen	Venez ici	Come here
Voici un exemple	Here's an example	Choisissez un symbole	Choose a symbol
A la page trois	On page three	Qui a fini?	Who's finished?
Voilà/Voici	Here is/are	Bien	Good
Répétez	Repeat	Très bien	Very good
Répondez	Answer	Excellent	Excellent
Ecrivez	Write	Bravo	Well done
Lisez	Read	Super	Super
Travaillez en groupes de quatre	Work in groups of four	En français	In French

GAMES AND ACTIVITIES

Activities with flashcards

- Give each student one flashcard representing a key phrase. This is what the student must listen for. Say the key phrases. Students put up their hands when they hear their key phrase. Increase the speed as you do this to maintain pace and so that students see it as a game.

- Students swap flashcards so that they get used to listening to more than one item. Say the key phrases in random order several times. Students count how many times their card is mentioned.

- Place each flashcard face down on the tables in the classroom, saying the appropriate key phrase as you do so. Then say one of the key phrases. A volunteer student tries to remember where that card is and turns over the card for the phrase.

- Show a flashcard and ask an either/or question, e.g. *Il aime jouer au football ou il aime aller à la piscine?* Students choose the correct statement.

- Take three or four cards. Show them to the students. Put each card in an envelope. Students remember which card is in which envelope. Shuffle the cards and see if they can work out which card is in which envelope now.

- Take the full set of flashcards. Flick quickly through the cards. Students say the key phrases for the cards which you showed.

Activities with the OHP

- Copy pictures or objects onto paper. You may find you can use illustrations on the flashcards as a 'template'. Cut them out and project their silhouettes on the OHP. Students identify the objects.

- Copy pictures onto OHT. Cut out each picture. Show the class the pictures and say the French for each picture as you show it. Cover the pictures with pieces of paper. Say a phrase to match a picture. Students come to the OHP and uncover the appropriate picture.

- Show a picture out of focus. Gradually bring the picture into focus. Students see how quickly they can give the key phrase to match the picture.

- Draw the trunk of a tree on an OHT. In the centre, write the start of a key phrase, e.g. *Je voudrais. . ./J'aime. . ./Il y a . . . .* Students come to the OHP and, using washable pens, write branches to complete the phrase, e.g. *Je voudrais. . . un hot-dog.*

Classroom activities

- *'Loto'* can be used to practise a wide range of language. Students each draw four or six squares. In each square they draw a symbol to represent a key phrase. Call out the key phrases in random order. Whenever students hear one of the phrases represented in their squares, they cover it up. When all their squares have been covered, they call *'Loto!'*.

- It is important to maintain concentration and pace as you ask students questions. Use some object, perhaps a dice or a ball, and then ask a question. Move quickly to a chosen student and place the object in front of the student. That student has to answer the question. Ask another question and give the object quickly to another student.

- This activity uses a 'magic' object. Students are only allowed to speak if they are holding the object. The sillier the object, the better. Students sit in a circle. You start off by holding the object and saying one of the key phrases, e.g. (from Unit 1) *J'ai un frère.* You then pass the object to the student next to you who says another phrase, e.g. *J'ai une sœur/ J'ai deux frères.* He/She passes the object to the next student, and so on. Each student should call out a different phrase. Continue in this way until the object returns to you.

HOW CAN FRENCH PLUS HELP YOU TO SURVIVE AN INSPECTION?

French Plus has been written to support teachers in meeting the criteria for inspection as stated by OFSTED. OFSTED assesses teaching and learning under three headings: **Standards of achievement**, **Quality of teaching** and **Quality of learning**. Below is a list of the main evidence sought under these criteria.

Standards of achievement

- Achievement is observed in all four skill areas (ATs)
- Students should use one skill to improve the quality of work in another, e.g. students listen to a conversation and use that as a basis for producing their own conversation.
- There is evidence of an increase in cultural awareness.

Quality of teaching

- Effective language teaching provides a highly organised sequence of planned activities.
- Teachers should create opportunities for students to practise their language skills as a class, in smaller groups and in pairs.
- There should be evidence of substantial use of the target language for all aspects of the lesson (see page 2).
- Assess pupils' work continuously, to include diagnostic assessment (see page 6).

Quality of learning

- Students should use the target language for genuine communication.
- Students should listen with keen concentration.
- Students should have access to authentic texts.

Accommodation

Teachers have enhanced the teaching rooms, open areas and corridors to promote learning and to improve the quality of the environment.

Methodology

'Effective language teaching provides a highly organised sequence of planned activities.' (OFSTED)

The learning of language in **French Plus** is based on the following steps of language learning:

1. **Setting clear objectives:** talk about the objectives with your students and make them aware of the importance of this business-like approach to learning.

   'The lessons have clear aims and purposes.' (OFSTED)

2. **Recognition:** the step where students meet new language for the first time. **French Plus** provides a variety of activities to check students' comprehension of new language. It is important that students really do feel confident about their understanding of new language before they are asked to use it.

3. **Repetition:** students cannot be expected to pronounce new language correctly, if they have not had the opportunity to repeat it after a model. **French Plus** provides a variety of short repetition tasks. Try repetition in groups, pairs and with individuals. Repetition should be based on understanding. Students should show that they understand what they are repeating by being selective in what they repeat. For example, students may repeat only the dialogue which matches a given visual or they may repeat only activities which they like. You will be required to pause the cassette for repetition activities.

4 **Production:** students show what they can do with the language which they have recognised, understood and repeated. They complete tasks based only on the language they have practised. These tasks show students that they can actually do something with the new language. As students experience this success they will be motivated to tackle the next unit with a positive attitude.

5 **Assessment:** the assessment of students' work should be linked directly to the learning objectives of the unit. You should remind students of the objectives and allow them to be involved in the process of self-assessment. The assessment in **French Plus** is an integral part of the teaching/learning process (see page 6).

Teaching listening

- Explain to students that they do not have to understand every word, to be able to answer questions.

- In most listening activities in **French Plus**, there is a series of recorded texts. Deal with each one separately. Allow pupils to listen to the recording again as you explain the answer, stopping the recording as appropriate. In this way students will learn gradually to gain confidence as they deal with each section. There should also be evidence of progression as they work through the activity. If you play all items at once and then go over the answers, the student who has failed to understand the first item will 'switch off' for the following items, and thereby experience failure and become demotivated.

Teaching speaking

- Students need as many opportunities as possible to practise speaking activities. Each student should be involved in at least one speaking activity in each lesson.

- Pair work is a useful tool for involving all students simultaneously in speaking activities and there are plenty of opportunities in **French Plus** for pair work. It needs, however, careful handling.

- Set clear tasks. Make sure all students understand the instructions before starting.

- Impose a time-limit – ten minutes absolute maximum. Be strict about it because students are skilled at pleading for more time!

- Do not allow students always to write out their dialogues. They cannot do this in assessment tasks and should not become too dependent on a written prop. A visual stimulus dialogue allows them the prompts they need. You will find such stimuli in **French Plus**.

- Tell students that some of them will be asked to perform their dialogues. This keeps them on task and makes them more accountable.

- Get students, when appropriate, to perform at the front of the class to overcome the problem of muttering into their books.

Teaching reading

Students need to acquire reading skills. As for listening, they must learn that they can answer questions without understanding every word of the text.

Teaching writing

- Copywriting tasks is an important part of the learning process. If students are asked to copywrite with a purpose, for example, by copying words under category headings, this very often improves their motivation.

- You can use the OHP to good effect. Get students to work in groups of four to produce a piece of writing which they then write on an overhead transparency, using soluble pens! Project the texts and use them as reading practice for the rest of the class.

- Writing offers an opportunity for students to use the computer. Many students will enjoy selecting a layout which suits their task. Students will also benefit from the ability to redraft work to produce the best possible outcome.

- Students' completed written work should be displayed to celebrate their achievement.

ASSESSMENT

'Assessments are used by teachers in their planning.' (OFSTED)

French Plus helps you to build regular assessment opportunities into lesson plans and classroom situations. Thus, assessment becomes an integral part of planning and practice.

The assessment worksheets can be used when students are ready to use them. They will help you to diagnose problems of individual students and thereby produce plans to support individual students' learning.

French Plus links directly with the NEAB's Certificate of Achievement. The assessment worksheets will act as the evidence that students have achieved the defined outcomes. These worksheets should be kept in a portfolio for each student.

The worksheets provided for speaking tasks do not need to be kept for evidence. For moderation purposes, at least 25% of the units for which certification is requested, must be supported by a tape recording of students' performances, for outcomes related to speaking.

To complete a unit successfully, a student must have achieved every outcome as specified in the NEAB syllabus. Individual outcomes may be attempted on more than one occasion and the evidence may be accumulated over time. **French Plus** offers students two worksheets for most outcomes to enable students to achieve the outcome through different tasks. Students can, however, re-do a worksheet if you think this would be desirable.

On some worksheets, students are tested on more items than are needed to achieve the outcome. Each outcome is stated clearly at the top of the worksheet. Check carefully what a student needs to do to achieve the outcome. For example, on Worksheet 10 (unit 2) students are tested on eleven prices. They need only, however, understand two of these to achieve the outcome.

On some worksheets, there are *Plus* additional activities indicated by ✚.

These are not assessed activities. They are follow-on activities for use in the classroom.

For information on the syllabus and procedures for the Certificate of Achievement in French, you should refer to the NEAB's publication which is obtainable from 31–33, Springfield Avenue, Harrogate, North Yorkshire HG1 2HW.

Transition to GCSE

Given that students may make sufficient progress during the course to be entered for GCSE, these materials and the NEAB's syllabus for the Certificate of Achievement have been designed to permit transfer between the two exams.

Students preparing for Foundation Tier GCSE will need to cover a wider range of topics and tasks than those found in **French Plus**. At the end of each unit in the Teacher's Book, there are notes of guidance on how to develop the unit further to prepare students for GCSE.

One way of preparing students who wish to progress to GCSE, is to complement units in **French Plus** with units in **Vital 1** and **Vital 2**, published by Collins Eduational. These books have been written especially to help students to achieve success in GCSE at Foundation Tier (grades C – G). Below is a chart of complementary units in **Vital**. You will need to check your GCSE syllabus to see which other units from **Vital** you will need to do in order to cover all the defined topics and tasks of your exam board.

For more information on **Vital**, please contact Collins Educational on 0141 306 3484 (telephone) or 0141 306 3750 (fax).

French Plus	Vital	French Plus	Vital
1	Vital 1, Unit 2	7	Vital 1, Unit 4
2	Vital 2, Unit 6	8	Vital 2, Unit 8
3	Vital 2, Unit 2	9	Vital 2, Unit 3
4	Vital 2, Unit 5	10	Vital 1, Unit 9
5	Vital 1, Unit 5	11	Vital 2, Unit 5
6	Vital 2, Units 8 + 13	12	Vital 1, Unit 10

Salut!

Objectives

- to give your name.
- to give your age.
- to talk about your family.
- to talk about your pets.

TEACHING NOTES

STUDENT'S BOOK, page 7
Objective 1: to give your name

Introduce this unit of work by stressing upon students the importance of being able to identify oneself when in France. Explain that French people carry a *carte d' identité* and discuss the current proposals in the UK for identity cards.

Explain that many French first names sound very similar to the English. Brainstorm students for examples of names that sound French, e.g. Louise. Explain that many names have a female form, e.g. *Louis/Louise*. Mention, too, that many French first names refer to saints, e.g. *Bernadette* and that French people have a Saint's Day as well as a birthday although Saint's Days are not always celebrated.

Look at the families on page 6 and brainstorm the class for any other famous families they can think of. Challenge them to find as many as they can in, say, one minute. Explain that families are usually referred to in French by using *les* plus the surname in the singular form, e.g. *Les Grimaldi* as opposed to The Smiths.

Background information

French people are issued with a *carte d'identité* at the age of 18 (*la majorité*). A person has to be 16 years of age to marry with parental con-sent, 18 years old to drive a car (but 16 to take lessons), and 18 to consume alcohol.

Presenting the language

Bring in pictures of famous pop stars/sports personalities. Distribute them to the students who take it in turns to stand up and introduce 'themselves', e.g. *Je m'appelle Damon Hill*. Encourage the use of *Salut* as well as *Bonjour*.

Classes which contain students who need more practice with this, could record them-selves individually, stating their own name or pretending to be someone else. You could then play the tape back to the class who decide whether the person on tape is telling the truth or not.

Activity 1
1 Je m'appelle Nicole.
2 Je m'appelle Colette.
3 Je m'appelle Sylvie.

Activity 2
1
– Bonjour, je m'appelle Sylvie.
– Bonjour, je m'appelle Caroline.
– Bonjour, je m'appelle Luc.
2
– Bonjour, je m'appelle Nicole.
– Bonjour, je m'appelle Julie.
– Bonjour, je m'appelle Sandrine.
– Bonjour, je m'appelle André.
3
– Bonjour, je m'appelle David.
– Bonjour, je m'appelle Eric.
– Bonjour, je m'appelle Marc.
– Bonjour, je m'appelle Anne-Marie.

Activity 3

Some students will need more practice of the question *Comment t'appelles-tu?*

Play the tape several times, pausing after this phrase for repetition practice. If students need further practice of this, go back to the pop stars/sports personalities pictures and repeat the exercise (students introduce 'themselves'), but extend it so that each student has to ask the next person *Comment t'appelles-tu?* before sitting down.

– Bonjour.
– Bonjour, comment t'appelles-tu?
– Je m'appelle Nicole. Et toi?

Activity 4

Differentiation Students who complete activity 4 while others are still working, could go on to either draw cartoons or find photos from magazines and then label them *Je m'appelle. . . .*

STUDENT'S BOOK, pages 8–9
Objective 2: to give your age

Presenting the language

Revise the numbers by playing bingo with cards which you or the students have made, using only numbers 1–20. Alternatively, give students a simple maths quiz by dividing the class into two teams and ask a question of each team (e.g. 2 + 2 =).

Give students plenty of opportunity to practise saying the numbers out of order (as opposed to parrot-fashion). Do this by having quick challenge games, e.g. place individual numbers at random on the OHP, cover one number and the first to guess wins.

Activity 1

Before beginning this activity explain that, as in the UK, French football teams have squad and not positional numbers. Look at the illustration of the football team and spend some time on the pronunciation of the players' names.

a
– Le numéro 13, c'est Dugarry.
– Le numéro 1, c'est. . .
– Le numéro 11, c'est. . .
– Le numéro 5, c'est. . .
– Le numéro 15, c'est. . .
– Le numéro 7, c'est. . .

b
– Je m'appelle Dugarry – numéro 13.
– Je m'appelle Desailly – numéro. . .
– Je m'appelle Guérin – numéro. . .
– Je m'appelle Zidane – numéro. . .
– Je m'appelle Karembeu – numéro. . .

Activity 2

This activity is followed by listening exercises for reinforcement of numbers.

a
– 3 4 6 9 11 15
b
– numéro 2
– numéro 6
– numéro 3
– numéro 12
– numéro 9
– numéro 16

c
– numéro 12
– numéro 6
– numéro 8
– numéro 9
– numéro 14
– numéro 11

Activity 3

Before starting this activity, revise numbers 1–20 with your students. Say the numbers and the students repeat after you.

Activity 4

Work on the key phrases for this activity but remind students that the main point of the activity is to give them practice with the numbers. Write the key words on the OHP/board and ask students for ideas using mime if necessary (e.g. *joueurs*).

a *Il y a onze joueuers dans une équipe de football. vrai (✓)*
b *Il y a six personnes dans le groupe Oasis. faux (✗)*

Differentiation Given a list of key phrases, more able students could make up further vrai/faux statements by simply substituting the key phrases given, e.g.

Il y a dans une équipe de rugby. . .
Il y a dans la classe de M. Smith. . .
Il y a dans le groupe Blur. . .

Activity 6

Practise the language actively by role-playing different situations/contexts in which students think they may be asked for their age, e.g. cinema/bus queue, etc. Students work in pairs, or groups of three, to mime a typical scene which would lead to the question *Quel âge as-tu?* and the answer *J'ai . . . ans*. The rest of the class has to guess the context.

Work part **a** of the activity orally with the students before getting them to write out the answers in the same form as the example.

Give them repetition practice for part **b** by playing the tape two or more times. The first time the students repeat the questions, the second time they repeat the answers. If they need further repetition practice, divide the class into two groups; one repeats the questions, the other repeats the answers and vice versa.

b
– Bonjour, comment t'appelles-tu?
– Je m'appelle Nicole. Et toi?
– Je m'appelle David. J'ai 16 ans. Quel âge as-tu?
– J'ai 15 ans.
– Moi, je m'appelle Colette. J'ai 16 ans!

Differentiation Some students may find this dialogue long. If so, offer them a strategy for breaking it down into manageable chunks:

– they tackle and practise the first question and answer only
– when they are confident with this, they add the second question and answer and the final statement.

More able students can copy out their dialogue based on the model.

Patterns of language

Explain that in French *j'ai*, meaning 'I have', is used when discussing age. Some students remember it by translating it as 'I have 15 years behind me'! Explain then that other forms of *avoir* have to be used when describing other people's age, e.g. *David a 16 ans/Quel âge as-tu?* Although students will not be assessed on *Il/Elle a. . .*, it could be useful to introduce it at this stage to the more able students.

STUDENT'S BOOK, page 10
Objective 3: to talk about your family

Presenting the language

Ask students to bring in photos of their brothers and sisters. Mix them up and then ask the students which photos belong to which students: *C'est la sœur de Darrell ou de Martin?* Move on then to ask the appropriate student *Comment s'appelle-t-il/elle?* – elicit a name only response at first and then encourage *Il/Elle s'appelle. . . .*

Practise *Quel âge a-t-il?* by using the famous people game again. Hold up the photographs one at a time and ask students *Quel âge a-t-il/elle?*. Students must be able to use *Il/Elle a . . .* to score the points.

Activity 1

Read through the flow chart with the students, making sure that they understand every sentence before playing the tape. Offer repetition practice by playing the tape several times, pausing to repeat the phrases that they find difficult. The questions often present more problems than the answers. If this is the case, get them to repeat the answers only at first, before repeating the whole dialogue. Students then copy out the phrases.

a
– Tu as des frères et des sœurs?
– J'ai un frère.
– J'ai une sœur.

– Comment s'appelle-t-il?
– Il s'appelle Luc.
– Comment s'appelle-t-elle?
– Elle s'appelle Julie.

– Quel âge a-t-il?
– Il a 15 ans.
– Quel âge a-t-elle?
– Elle a 2 ans.

Differentiation   More able students could copy out the question phrases again and, using the model, write in the correct information to describe their own brothers and sisters.

For further practice of this, do a class survey on the OHP or board to show whether the class has more sisters or brothers. Start off the questioning: *Becky, tu as des frères et des sœurs?* and mark off the response (or get another student to do this) in bar chart form.

Exploit students' knowledge of their favourite idols with the game *Qui est-ce?* They give a description, e.g. *J'ai quatre frères et une sœur.* The rest of the class has to guess who it is.

Activity 2
1 Je m'appelle Colette.
2 J'ai un frère. Il s'appelle Albert.
3 Il a 18 ans.
4 J'ai une sœur. Elle s'appelle Stéphanie
5 Elle a 12 ans.

STUDENT'S BOOK, page 11
Objective 4: to talk about your pets

Presenting the language

Use mime to present new vocabulary and play games on the OHP or with flashcards to practise it, e.g. Kim's game: display animal flashcards or animal outlines on OHT, but leave one out. Students have to decide quickly which one it is.

Activity 1

If they need further practice with this, use other selective repetition techniques, e.g. they repeat only the animals they have.

1 J'ai un hamster.   4 J'ai un lapin.
2 J'ai un chien.   5 J'ai un chat.
3 J'ai un oiseau.   6 J'ai un poisson.

Practise *Tu as. . ?* by doing animal 'interviews'. Students work in pairs and interview every other student in the class about whether they have a given animal (they take it in turns to ask the question/record the response). Eventually every pair has information about how many dogs/cats/hamsters, etc. the class has. They can do a design to illustrate this, e.g. a fish with seven bubbles coming from its mouth, each

containing a person's name. The design can be displayed.

Activity 2

Some students may not want to repeat the phrases in the 'correct' voice. Do not push this – the main aim is to give them practice at the language, not at being impressionists!

Tu as des animaux?
A Oui, j'ai deux hamsters.
B Non, je n'ai pas d'animaux.
C Oui, j'ai un chien.

Differentiation   Some students may have more difficulty with *Je n'ai pas d'animaux.* Give them opportunities to practise this with mime; the images produced sometimes help them to retain more abstract concepts more easily.

Patterns of language

Explain that *J'ai un poisson* becomes *Je n'ai pas de. . .* when in the negative form. Give them a tip about plurals: most nouns simply take an 's' to form the plural, but there are some exceptions, e.g. *animaux.*

TRANSITION TO GCSE

For GCSE, students will need to build upon the language of the unit, so that they can:

● describe people's hair.
   Il/Elle a les cheveux (+ colour)
                            (+ adjective)

● describe people's eyes.
   Il/Elle a les yeux (+ colour)

● describe how people look.
   Il/Elle est grand(e), petit(e), gros(se), mince.

● describe people's personality.
   Il/Elle est calme, intelligent(e), sympa, etc.

Check your GCSE syllabus for the complete list. Remember that students need not learn all the words from the list for active use. Tell students to choose two or three adjectives from the list which they find easy to learn. These are the words which they should use in their speaking and writing exams.

Tell them that they will have to recognise and understand the other words, but that they will not be forced to write them or say them.

When teaching the adjectives, do not worry about adjective agreement. Remember that for Foundation Tier, students can communicate successfully despite such errors.

Further practice on this topic can be found in **Vital 2**, *Unité 2*.

USE OF ASSESSMENT WORKSHEETS

Worksheet 1

Dialogue A
– Bonjour. Comment t'appelles-tu?
– Je m'appelle Julie.
– Ah, bonjour, Julie. Quel âge as-tu?
– Eh bien, j'ai 16 ans.
– 16 ans. . . moi aussi. Dis-moi, Julie, tu as des frères et des sœurs?
– Oui, j'ai deux frères. Ils s'appellent Mathieu et Martin.
– Quel âge ont-ils?
– Mathieu a dix ans et Martin, il a cinq ans.
– Tu as aussi des sœurs?
– Non, je n'ai pas de sœurs. . . malheureusement!
– Tu as des animaux?
– Oui, j'ai un lapin et un hamster. Et toi, tu as des animaux?

Dialogue B
– Salut. Tu t'appelles comment?
– Je m'appelle Thomas.
– Salut, Thomas! Quel âge as-tu?
– J'ai 15 ans.
– Moi aussi. Dis-moi, as-tu des frères et des sœurs?
– Oui, j'ai un frère et une sœur. Mon frère s'appelle Jo.
– Il a quel âge?
– Il a 18 ans.
– Et ta sœur, quel âge a-t-elle?
– Véronique a 9 ans.
– Tu as des animaux?

– Oui, j'ai deux chiens, cinq poissons et trois chats.
– Deux chiens, cinq poissons et trois chats! C'est beaucoup, hein?

Worksheet 2

Bonjour. Comment t'appelles-tu?
– Je m'appelle Marie.
– Ah, salut, Marie. Quel âge as-tu?
– J'ai 14 ans.
– 14 ans. . . moi, aussi. Dis-moi, Marie, tu as des frères et des sœurs?
– Oui, j'ai un frère et une sœur. Mon frère s'appelle David.
– Quel âge a-t-il?
– David a 2 ans.
– Et ta sœur, quel âge a-t-elle?
– Nicole a 11 ans!
– 11. . . ah, mon frère a 11 ans aussi! Tu as des animaux, Marie?
– Oui, j'ai un lapin, un poisson et un oiseau.

Worksheet 3

If students have problems achieving the tasks, allow them to return to them on a later occasion.

Worksheet 4

Activity 2 is not for assessment, but can be used as a follow on activity in class.

ANSWERS FOR ASSESSMENT WORKSHEETS

Worksheet 1
Julie: 16, 2 brothers, 10 and 5, no sisters, rabbit and hamster.
Thomas: 15, 1 brother, 18, 1 sister, 9, 2 dogs, 5 fish, 3 cats.

Worksheet 2
1 b; 2 a; 3 c; 4 c; 5 a; 6 d; 7 rabbit, fish, bird.

Worksheet 4
1 c; 2 a.

Worksheet 6
A: a sister; Anne; 11; a brother; is called Martin; is 6; 15; cat; rabbit.
B: I'm 16; 1 brother called Paul; 13; I've got a sister; is 11; 2 dogs; a cat; 3 birds; 6 fish.

Au café

Objectives

- to understand a café menu.
- to order a snack and a drink.
- to ask for and pay the bill.

TEACHING NOTES

STUDENT'S BOOK, page 13

Introduce this unit of work by explaining to students that they are going to learn the language they will need to survive independently in a French café situation, i.e. they will be able to order a snack and a drink from the menu and ask for and pay the bill. Stress that it is a café situation, not a formal resaurant, and explain the difference. Go on to describe the other types of eating places in France (see background information) and ask for comparisons with the British pub/types of eating places in the UK.

Explain to students that there is an accepted practice in France for ordering from the waiter/ paying the bill and that they will learn about this and any other important customs or 'rules' as they work through the unit.

Background information

The old saying that the French live to eat is still very much the case today. In spite of the fact that availability of *le fast food* is spreading at an alarming rate, the French still have a reputation for being lovers of good food and wines. Meals are a focus for family life and although it is less common these days for families to eat together at lunch time (due to distances to school/work, shorter lunch break, etc.), the evening meal at the table is still very important to most families. School meals and lunches *à la cantine*, however, are often much more elaborate affairs than in the UK; a typical example would include three courses from a variety of choices, and wine for adults. There are a variety of eating places in France including *brasseries* (cafés with more extensive menus), *crêperies* (pancake houses), *pizzerias, salons de thé* (increasingly popular) and, of course, in bigger towns a McDonald's (McDo) which is very popular with the young. Restaurants are more formal, and usually more expensive; there is usually the choice of a set menu (*menu à prix fixe*) which is often three courses from a limited selection or the *à la carte* menu which offers a wider variety of dishes at individual prices. There is, of course, *la carte des vins*, offering a range of wines. It is not unusual for large supermarkets or hypermarkets to have a restaurant, and although they are often run on a *le self* basis, they are quite formal.

STUDENT'S BOOK, page 14
Objective 1: to understand a café menu

Presenting the language

Introduce the vocabulary, using flashcards or realia. Present the cognates first, moving on to the less obvious later.

Consolidate with usual reinforcement techniques:

Show flashcards/realia in turn, asking questions, e.g. *C'est un coca?*, to elicit a *oui/non* response, then go on to look for alternative answers, e.g. *Non, c'est un orangina.*

Give out flashcards/realia to individuals and ask for items back, e.g. *Un coca, s'il vous plaît.*

Play games on the OHP, e.g. place pictures of an item on the OHP, switch on and off giving only a glimpse of the snack or drink. The first to guess wins. Alternatively, you could begin to draw an item and the first to guess what it is wins.

Play the tasting game. Blindfold students and let them taste one of the drinks/snacks. They then say in French what it is.

Spend some time on pronunciation before playing the tape. Discourage students from reverting back to the English pronunciation of the cognates.

Activity 1
b

A Je voudrais un café, s'il vous plaît.
B Je voudrais un hot-dog, s'il vous plaît.
C Je voudrais une pizza, s'il vous plaît.
D Je voudrais un coca, s'il vous plaît.
E Je voudrais une bière, s'il vous plaît.

Activity 2

This is a further recognition exercise.
b

– Marc?
– Je voudrais un orangina et un hot-dog.
– Pour Marc, un orangina et un hot-dog. Sophie?
– Je voudrais des frites et un thé au lait.
– Pour Sophie, des frites et un thé au lait. Philippe?
– Je voudrais un coca et une pizza.
– Pour Philippe, un coca et une pizza. Hélène?
– Je voudrais un sandwich au jambon et un café-crème.
– Pour Hélène, un sandwich au jambon et un café-crème.

Activity 3

If students need further repetition practice, play the tape again and use a different selective repetition technique, e.g. half the class repeats the drinks only, the other half repeats the snacks.

– Un coca.
– Un orangina.
– Une bière.
– Un café crème.
– Un thé au lait.
– Un hot-dog.
– Une pizza.
– Des frites.
– Un sandwich au jambon.

Activity 4

This activity provides an opportunity for pupils to practise writing and translating the new vocabulary. This activity could be extended or modified so that the list headings were different, e.g. *à manger/à boire, chaud/fraud,* etc.

Differentiation Students who have difficulty writing, could use pictures cut out from magazines and, having had the headings explained and/or written out for them, they demonstrate comprehension by sticking the right pictures into the right column. (You will need a good supply of pictures or drawings for this.) More able students who finish the exercises early, could then go on to begin a café phrase book for adults. (They could add to it later.) At this stage, they simply make a booklet by folding six sheets of A5 paper in half and writing on each page one French word (or illustrating it with pictures or drawings) and its meaning in English.

Patterns of language

Point out that in French some words are masculine and some are feminine, e.g. *un coca, une bière.* Explain that, at this stage, it is not disastrous to get the gender wrong – the main aim is to learn the vocabulary for the snacks and drinks. (For assessment purposes, gender does not have to be correct.)

STUDENT'S BOOK, pages 15–16
Objective 2: to order a snack and a drink

Presenting the language

Introduce *Je voudrais. . .* by using the flashcards/realia once again. Give items out and ask for

them back, using *Je voudrais. . .*, and elicit meaning. Practise the pronunciation of *Je voudrais. . .* and then get students to use it to ask you for an item. When all students have an

---

item, get them to swap by asking for items from each other. When students are comfortable with *Je voudrais. . .*, repeat the exercise adding *s'il vous plaît*. If students have difficulty retaining *s'il vous plaît*, play a game of 'Simon says' using classroom language and substituting *s'il vous plaît* for 'Simon says', e.g. *Asseyez vous!/ Asseyez-vous, s'il vous plaît*. When they are comfortable with *s'il vous plaît*, explain that it is useful for attracting the attention of the waiter/waitress, e.g. *Madame, s'il vous plaît*. (Clicking fingers or calling out loud is unacceptable.)

Introduce *Vous désirez?* by role-playing the café situation with, say, three students and you as *serveur/serveuse*. Eventually swap roles so that students play the role of the waiter/waitress.

Activity 1
1 Bonjour. Vous désirez?
2 Je voudrais un hot-dog, s'il vous plaît
3 Je voudrais une bière, s'il vous plaît.
4 Je voudrais un coca, s'il vous plaît.

Before beginning activity 2, read through the flow chart with students for pronunciation practice. Let students take turns reading out a sentence on their own.

Activity 2

When students are confident with their new dialogue they can 'perform' it for the rest of the class. It could then be recorded on tape or video. This will improve motivation and reveal their social skills, i.e. you can check for appropriate behaviour while awaiting the order or tone of voice when catching the attention of the waiter/waitress, etc. Use props such as a tray, tea towel, ordering pad, glasses, etc. for a more authentic and atmospheric café.

Differentiation   More able students could now add *Je voudrais. . .* and *s'il vous plaît* to their phrase book.

a
– Bonjour. Vous désirez?
– Je voudrais un hot-dog, s'il vous plaît.
– Je voudrais une bière, s'il vous plaît.
– Je voudrais un coca, s'il vous plaît.

Differentiation   Some students may be happier inventing their new dialogues in pairs at first. Let them do this and then encourage them to join with another pair. If they need more practice, give each student a flashcard to prompt their order. This will also avoid overuse of the cognates. More able students could write out their new dialogue or produce a photo story by bringing in photos of themselves and adding speech bubbles to it.

Activity 3
Depending on the ability of the class, students could either copy this dialogue out and fill the gaps by reading the speech bubbles in the photo, or they could copy it, close their books and fill in the gaps by listening to the tape (activity 2).

Activity 4
Use the illustration to reinforce all the language learned so far:

● Students play Kim's game in pairs. One pupil covers up to five words with strips of paper and the others have to guess which are 'missing' in one minute.

● Students work in pairs to time each other, asking politely (*Je voudrais. . . , s'il vous plaît*) for every item on the counter.

● Students work in pairs; one orders, one takes the order.

Differentiation   More able pupils could close their textbook and attempt to write the order from memory. They could then check their own spellings when they have finished taking the order.

Activity 5
Brainstorm ideas for a child menu and get pupils to either write out one of their choice or to make one on the computer. More able pupils may ask you for vocabulary that is not in this unit, so be prepared for this. Examples you could give might include *un gateau, une glace* or *un fruit* but remember that they will not be assessed on these.

Objective 3: to ask for and pay the bill

Activity 1

Before beginning this activity, practise the numbers 1–20 (see Student's Book, pages 8–9 and Teacher's Book, page 8 for ideas). Practise prices (1F–20F in whole francs only) by holding up a flashcard/realia in one hand, a price tag in the other and by asking *C'est combien?* Students then look at the menu and listen to a read-through of the items with prices on tape. Play the tape again, pausing after each item so that students can repeat. If students need further practice of this, play the tape two or three more times and use different repetition techniques, e.g. pause the tape before the price is given – pupils repeat the item, read out its price and then repeat the price after the tape.

– Boissons
– Un coca 10f
– Un orangina 10f
– Une bière 12f
– Un café 6 f
– Un café crème 8 f
– Un thé au lait 7f
– Snacks
– Un hot-dog 12f
– Une pizza 20f
– Un sandwich au jambon 10f
– Des frites 12f

Activity 2

Differentiation   More able pupils who finish quickly could work out the bill for each of the orders and write this next to the order. Alternatively they could go back to their phrase book and add a price conversion at the back. (You may have to give them this on the OHP/board.)

– Marc?
– Je voudrais une pizza et un coca, s'il vous plaît.
– Pour Marc, une pizza et un coca. Hélène?
– Je voudrais un café et un hot-dog.
– Pour Hélène, un café et un hot-dog. Philippe?
– Je voudrais un orangina et des frites.
– Pour Philippe, un orangina et des frites. Sophie?
– Je voudrais un sandwich au jambon et un thé au lait.
– Pour Sophie, un sandwich au jambon et un thé au lait.

Activity 3

A
– Un coca, c'est combien?
– Un coca, c'est 10 francs.
– 10 francs?
– Oui, 10 francs.

B
– Un thé au lait, c'est combien?
– Un thé au lait, c'est 7 francs.
– 7 francs?
– Oui, 7 francs.

C
– Une bière, c'est combien?
– Une bière, c'est 12 francs.
– 12 francs?
– Oui, 12 francs.

D
– Un orangina, c'est combien?
– Un orangina, c'est 10 francs.
– 10 francs?
– Oui, 10 francs.

E
– Un café crème, c'est combien?
– Un café crème, c'est 8 francs.
– 8 francs?
– Oui, 8 francs.

Activity 4

Introduce *L'addition, s'il vous plaît* and play the tape to allow students the opportunity to practise it. Reinforce it through role-play. Students work in pairs. One has a flashcard/picture (or more depending on the ability of the pair) and asks *L'addition, s'il vous plaît.* The other student finds the price(s) from the menu, repeats the item(s) and gives the price(s), e.g. *Un coca, 10 francs.*

a
– L'addition, s'il vous plaît.
– Oui. . ., un hot-dog, 12 francs, et un thé au lait, 7 francs, ça fait 19 francs.
– 19 francs?
– Oui, 19 francs.

Differentiation   Less able students will probably find it difficult to cope with more than one item at first. Give them plenty of practice with this and, if possible, let them move on to two items, using a pencil and piece of paper to work out the bill first. Meanwhile very able students could go back to the dialogue they performed earlier in the unit and add this new dimension to it. If their original role-play was recorded on video, this could now be extended. Mention the practice of using tabs for each round of drinks – they could incorporate this into the role-play.

Activity 5

Brainstorm with students the type of foods that will be appropriate to each of the situations. Write up suggestions on the OHP/board. Before beginning the dialogues, the students could draw a grid with three columns (*Végétarienne/Gourmand(e)/20 francs*) and put the appropriate foods in the right column. They will then feel more able to get on with the task of writing up the dialogues.

Differentiation   Less able pupils may need you to give them one model dialogue from which to work. You could write this out and photocopy it and then work with them in a small group to help them with adapting it. Alternatively, you could write out a list of phrases for one of the dialogues which they then have to arrange in the right order. This would then serve as a model for the other two exercises.

TRANSITION TO GCSE

In this unit, students have learnt the main phrases needed to order a meal. They will need, however, to extend their vocabulary of items of food and drink (see individual GCSE syllabus).

In addition, they will need to be able to:

- ask if food and drink is available.
  Avez-vous. . . ?
- ask for a fixed price menu.
  Le menu à . . . F, s'il vous plaît.
- ask for an explanation of something on the menu.
  Un croque-monsieur, c'est quoi?
- express opinions about food.
  J'aime. . .
  Je n'aime pas. . .
- express opinions about a meal.
  C'était. . .
- accept/decline offers of food and drink.
  Merci, non.
  Oui, s'il vous plaît.

- ask where the toilet or telephone is.
  Le téléphone, s'il vous plaît?
  Les toilettes, s'il vous plaît?

For each GCSE task, find the simplest possible French. Candidates do not score extra marks for longer sentences in role-plays. Thus, *Les toilettes, s'il vous plaît?* gains as many marks as *Où sont les toilettes, s'il vous plaît?*

To help students to learn all the items of food and drink required on the GCSE syllabus, group the words as you teach them. For example, teach students firstly words which look similar to English words, e.g. *le melon, le steak grillé, le porc, la salade.*

Remember to allow students plenty of opportunity to practise repeating the words after you or after a recording. Correct pronunciation is important for effective communication at GCSE.

Further practice on this topic can be found in **Vital 2**, *Unité 6.*

USE OF ASSESSMENT WORKSHEETS

Worksheet 9
1
Dialogue 1
– Bonjour, madame. Vous désirez?
– Je voudrais un sandwich au jambon, s'il vous plaît.

– Un sandwich au jambon. Oui, madame, et avec ça?
– Mm. . . un café crème, s'il vous plaît.
– Alors. . . un sandwich au jambon et un café crème. Tout de suite, madame.

Dialogue 2

– Bonjour, monsieur.
– Bonjour, madame. La carte, s'il vous plaît.
– Oui, monsieur.
– Vous avez choisi, monsieur?
– Oui, une pizza et des frites, s'il vous plaît.
– Une pizza-frites. Oui, monsieur, et avec ça?
– Un orangina, s'il vous plaît.
– Alors, une pizza-frites et un orangina. Oui, monsieur.

2

Dialogue 1

– Bonjour, madame. Vous désirez?
– Je voudrais un hot-dog, s'il vous plaît.
– Un hot-dog. Oui, madame, et avec ça?
– Mm...une bière, s'il vous plaît.
– Alors. . . un hot-dog et une bière. Tout de suite, madame.

Dialogue 2

– Bonjour, monsieur. Vous désirez?
– Un coca et un thé au lait, s'il vous plaît.
– Un coca et un thé au lait. C'est tout?
– Oui, c'est tout.
– Tout de suite, Monsieur.

Worksheet 10

Point out to students that the prices are repeated during the recording. Tell them that this often happens in conversations and is something we use to help us to understand.

– Alors, vous avez la carte?
– Oui.
– Ecoutez. Voici les prix d'aujourd'hui. Vous écrivez les prix sur la carte, d'accord? Alors, les snacks. . . un hot-dog. . . 15 francs.

– 15 francs. . . et un sandwich au jambon, c'est combien?
– Un sandwich au jambon . . . 14 francs.
– 14 francs. . . et des frites?
– Des frites. . . 12 francs.
– 12 francs. . . . Et une pizza?
– Une pizza, c'est 15 francs.
– 15 francs. . . . Et maintenant les boissons. . . .
– Oui, les boissons. Alors, un coca. . . 10 francs.
– Un coca. . . 10 francs.
– Un orangina. . . 11 francs.
– Un orangina . . . 11F.
– Une bière. . . 10 francs.
– Une bière. . . 10 francs.
– Un café crème, 12 francs et un thé au lait, 13 francs.
– Alors, 12 francs pour un café crème. . . et 13 francs pour un thé au lait.
– Oui, c'est ça. Vous avez tous les prix?
– Oui.
– Bien, merci.

Worksheet 11

Students take it in turns to unravel the puzzle for each person.

Activity 2 is not an assessed task.

Worksheet 12

Discuss the symbols with the class before students start working in pairs. It is important that students know exactly what they have to do before they start on the task.

Worksheets 15 and 16

Students could use the computer to create attractive menus.

ANSWERS FOR ASSESSMENT WORKSHEETS

Worksheet 9

1 Marie: ham sandwich and coffee.
   Paul: pizza and chips and orangina.
2 Nicole: hot-dog and beer.
   David: coca-cola and tea.

Worksheet 10

hot-dog 15F, sandwich au jambon 14F, frites 12F, pizza 15F, un coca 10F, orangina 11F, bière 10F, café crème 12F, thé au lait 13F.

Worksheet 13

Drinks: coca-cola, beer, orangina, white coffee, tea with milk.
Snacks: pizza, hot-dog, chips, ham sandwich.

Worksheet 14

thé au lait 10F, bière 14F, orangina 12F, café crème 14F, sandwich au jambon 15F, hot-dog 12F, chips 11f, pizza 16F.

Au collège

Objectives

- to talk about the school subjects you do.
- to express an opinion about school subjects.
- to write your own school timetable.

TEACHING NOTES

STUDENT'S BOOK, page 19

Discuss the objectives with your students, pointing out that when they have completed this unit they will be able to talk about these aspects of their school life in French.

Make comparisons of subjects studied/typical timetables/the school week/school holiday patterns (see background information) in France and the UK.

Background information

School is compulsory in France between the ages of six and sixteen. All education is controlled by the state and most schools are free and non-religious. There are, however, private schools run on a religious basis where fees are paid. Although children do not have to go to school until the age of six, many go to a nursery school (*la maternelle*) where they learn very basic numeracy and literacy from the age of two.

Primary school (*l'école primaire*) lasts for five years and then children go to a secondary school (*le collège/lycée*) between the ages of eleven and sixteen. Many students continue in education to the age of eighteen, when they will either take the *baccalauréat* examination (which is very academic and which allows them to go on to a university) or a technical or vocational diploma depending upon the type of institution they have attended since the age of sixteen.

School hours in France are long (8 a.m. to 4 p.m. or 5 p.m.) and students have a lot of homework to do in the evenings. Although Wednesday afternoons are free, many students have to go to school on a Saturday morning.

Young children whose parents work late, usually have the chance to stay behind at school in the *garderie* until about 6.30 p.m. School children in France do not have to wear a uniform.

STUDENT'S BOOK, page 20
Objective 1: to talk about the school subjects you do

Presenting the language

Using flashcards, present the vocabulary for the school subjects. Go on to use the OHP (see the section on the use of the OHP) and possibly props (a globe for geography, ball for sport, etc.) for reinforcement activities.
Play picture lotto with cards you have made yourself or other games, e.g. 'Mind-reader'; one

student has to think of a subject and the rest of the class guesses what it is.

Activity 1

– Exemple: Je m'appelle Colette. Aujourd'hui, je fais français.
– Je m'appelle Sylvie. Aujourd'hui, je fais technologie.
– Je m'appelle Nicole. Aujourd'hui, je fais maths.
– Je m'appelle Paul. Aujourd'hui, je fais musique.

– Je m'appelle Luc. Aujourd'hui, je fais anglais.
– Je m'appelle Pascale. Aujourd'hui, je fais sciences.
– Je m'appelle Laure. Aujourd'hui, je fais géographie.
– Je m'appelle Simon. Aujourd'hui, je fais dessin.
– Je m'appelle David. Aujourd'hui, je fais sport.
– Je m'appelle Anne. Aujourd'hui, je fais histoire.

If you feel students need more recognition/repetition practice, tell them to repeat only the subjects they studied at primary school, for example. They could then finish this activity by repeating all of the subjects in small groups after the tape.

Activity 2

Before tackling this activity, revise *aujourd'hui* and *demain*. Write that day's date on the board to illustrate *aujourd'hui* and the following day's date for *demain*.

Introduce *Que fais-tu au collège aujourd'hui?* by playing a game of spin-the-bottle (or a similar game where students are chosen at random to answer a question). Divide the class into groups and spin a bottle in the middle of the group, repeating the question several times. The group then chants the question in time with the bottle, until it stops spinning. The person the bottle points to has to name one

subject that the class does that day, e.g. *Aujourd'hui, je fais. . .* They then spin the bottle and the game continues until everyone has had a chance to name a subject. When you feel that students can ask the question with some degree of confidence, move on to activity 3.

Activity 3

a
– Que fais-tu au collège aujourd'hui?
– Moi, je fais maths et sciences. Et toi?
– Je fais français et histoire.

Differentiation Some students may have difficulty adapting the dialogue. If this is the case, copy the dialogue onto an OHT and underline the words which students need to change in order to talk about the subjects they do that day. Work out with the students how the sentences need to be adapted and practise the adapted sentences in a group. Move on so that students are practising the dialogue in pairs and gradually erase parts of the dialogue on the OHP so that students are eventually working from memory. Students then write out their new dialogue.

STUDENT'S BOOK, page 21
Objective 2: to express an opinion about school subjects

Presenting the language

Before beginning activity 1, explain to students that they are going to learn to say whether they like/dislike or love/hate the various subjects. Play the Emperor Nero game: ask students to consider their feelings about each of the school subjects as you read them aloud in French and to put their thumbs up or down according to their opinion. Have a 'thumbometer' to determine popularity of subjects.

Give out photos of famous personalities. Students have to stand up and say which subject they think this person would like, e.g. *Je m'appelle Eric Cantona. J'aime le sport* (Jill Dando – *la géographie*, Vanessa Paradis – *la musique*, etc.).

Practise *J'aime. . .* and *J'adore. . .* thoroughly before moving onto the negative expressions. To practise the negative expressions, e.g. *Je*

n'aime pas. . . and *Je déteste. . .*, which low-ability students often find difficult, play a lie-detector game. Students work in groups and write down a subject that they dislike. The group leader either reads correctly what is on the paper or calls bluff. The rest of the class decides if the statement is *vrai ou faux*.

Before starting activity 1, work through the flow chart with the students. Get them to then work with a partner to use each of the expressions once.

Activity 1

Before playing the tape, draw a grid on the OHP (it is better to have prepared this beforehand) to show the school subjects in one column, with two further columns (Paul/Claudette) which students tick on listening to the tape. Get students to copy this grid.

a

– Je m'appelle Paul. J'aime les maths, le français et le sport.
– Je m'appelle Claudette. Moi, j'aime les sciences, la musique et la technologie.
  J'aime aussi l'anglais.

Write the gapped dialogue on the OHP/ board:
Tu aimes quelles matières?
J'aime . . . et . . . . Je n'aime pas . . . . Et toi?
J'adore . . . . Je déteste . . . .

Ask students to copy out the dialogue and to fill in the gaps from the tape.

b

– Tu aimes quelles matières?
– J'aime les maths et les sciences. Je n'aime pas le dessin. Et toi?
– J'adore le dessin. Je déteste l'anglais.

Differentiation   Some students may have difficulty in writing or copying the names of the subjects at the same time as listening to the tape. Allow them to substitute symbols at first and then ask them to copy out the whole sentence later. More able students could add a further column and, working in pairs, could tick the subjects that their partner says he or she likes.

Activity 2

1
– Tu aimes le sport?
– Oui, j'aime le sport.

2
– Tu aimes l'histoire?
– Non, je n'aime pas l'histoire.

3
– Tu aimes le dessin?
– Non, je déteste le dessin.

4
– Tu aimes les maths?
– Oui, j'aime les maths.

5
– Tu aimes la géographie?
– Non, je n'aime pas la géographie.

6
– Tu aimes la musique?
– Oui, j'adore la musique.

Differentiation   Those who copy out the grid much more quickly than other students, could listen to the exercise with headphones. They could then make a *matières* wordsearch for those who are still working.

Activity 3

When students have collected their information, they can illustrate their results in a graph. They could present the information in a more original way, for example, by drawing a rugby ball/castle, etc. and writing in it the number of people who like sport/history.

Patterns of language

Explain *J'aime. . .* and *Tu aimes. . .*, pointing out that the 's' in *aimes* is not pronounced; therefore, it sounds just the same as in *J'aime . . . .* Demonstrate on the OHP/board how *Tu aimes. . .* can be used to ask a question by simply adding a question mark and changing the tone of voice. More able students who may go on to GCSE could also be introduced to *Il/Elle aime. . . .* As a homework activity, they could find their own pictures and make captions, e.g. *Celine Dion – elle aime la musique.*

STUDENT'S BOOK, pages 22–23
Objective 3: to write your own school timetable

Presenting the language

It is crucial for students to know the days of the week if they are going to work on timetable exercises, so spend as much time as necessary on this. Lower ability students usually retain new language more easily if they learn it to a rhythm, tapping on desks or inventing a rap. Use *aujourd'hui/demain* to reinforce the days

out of sequence. Call out *Aujourd'hui c'est lundi, demain c'est. . .*, etc. The first to answer wins and eventually more able students will be able to lead the exercise.

Activity 1

When students are confident with the days and able to use them out of sequence, begin activity 1.

a

- lundi
- mardi
- mercredi
- jeudi

- vendredi
- samedi
- dimanche

b

a – mardi – c'est 2
b – lundi
c – vendredi
d – mercredi
e – jeudi

c

- lundi
- mardi
- mercredi
- jeudi

- vendredi
- samedi
- dimanche

Activity 3

Work through the flow chart with the whole class. Then ask students to volunteer statements using *Je fais* + subject + day. To avoid monotony, students could make true or false statements and the rest of the class could try to catch them out. When they have had plenty of practice with this, move onto the question form. Give several examples before asking the students to work on this in pairs. Eventually move on to activity 3c. Challenge students to write more than ten sentences!

Differentiation More able students could close their books and work from memory on activity 3b. Very able students could attempt to write the sentences from memory.

Activity 4

Work this exercise orally first so that all students are comfortable with it before attempting the questions. Ask students to copy out the questions and to answer them in English. More able students who finish early could then make up true/false statements for their partner.

Activity 6

There are obviously no conclusive answers for this exercise, but it is worth brainstorming with students the subjects they think each person has passed.

Activity 7

It may be helpful to provide blank timetables for your students. More able students may be able to complete the whole timetable. Students could then go on to describe their *journée idéale* or to word-process their timetable in French on the computer.

Patterns of language

Explain to students that *le mardi* is used for 'on Tuesdays' and that an 's' should not be added to *mardi*!

To round off this unit of work, you could have a 'pub quiz' with your students about their school life. Divide the class into two teams and ask the students questions pertinent to that class, for example:

Comment s'appelle le professeur de géographie?
Tu as combien de leçons de maths par semaine?

The passive vocabulary will be more extensive so you may have to mime. Remember that students will not be assessed on this language.

TRANSITION TO GCSE

The language of the unit forms a sound basis for the topic of school at GCSE. In addition, students will need to be able to:

- describe when and how they travel to and from school.
  Comment vas-tu au collège?
  à pied/à vélo/en voiture/en bus/en train/en métro

- describe when school begins and ends.
  La journée commence/finit à quelle heure?
  La journée commence à neuf heures.
  La journée finit à trois heures et demie.

- describe how many lessons there are.
  Il y a combien de cours?
  Il y a cinq cours.

- describe how long they last.
  Ils durent combien de minutes?
  Cinquante minutes.

- describe break times and lunchtimes.
  La récréation (le déjeuner) est à quelle heure?
  A . . . heure (s).
  Qu'est-ce que tu fais pendant la récréation?
  Je joue au foot.
  Je fais mes devoirs.

- describe homework.
  Tu as des devoirs?
  J'ai deux heures de devoirs.

In addition, students must be able to ask for and give details of extra-curricular activities. These will be covered in Unit 6 of **French Plus**.

The topic of school is quite a full topic at GCSE, but the greatest emphasis will probably be on subjects studied which students have already covered in **French Plus**. The additional tasks can be completed successfully if students firstly recognise the question and secondly give as short an answer as possible.

Remember, students do not need to answer in full sentences to communicate effectively.

Further practice on this topic can be found in **Vital 2**, *Unité 2*.

USE OF ASSESSMENT WORKSHEETS

Worksheet 17
1
– Le jeudi, tu fais quelles matières, Jeanne?
– Le jeudi. . .alors le premier cours, c'est sciences.
– Ah, oui. . . et après ça?
– On a français et anglais.
– Français et anglais. Tu aimes l'anglais, Jeanne?
– Oui, j'aime bien l'anglais.
– Et le quatrième et le cinquième cours?
– On a deux heures de technologie. Et après, c'est l'heure du déjeuner.
– Alors, qu'est ce que tu fais l'après-midi?
– L'après-midi, on a trois cours. Le premier, c'est histoire, puis, on a deux heures de dessin. J'aime bien le dessin et c'est bien pour finir la journée.

Worksheet 18
– Et tu aimes quelles matières, Michel?
– J'aime beaucoup le français et j'adore la technologie!
– C'est vrai, tu adores la technologie?
– Oui, bien sûr. J'aime le français et j'aime beaucoup la technologie. Ce sont des matières très intéressantes.

– Et. . . est-ce qu'il y a des matières que tu n'aimes pas?
– Je n'aime pas tellement la musique. . . et je déteste les sciences!
– Tu déteste les sciences? Pourquoi?
– Parce que les sciences, c'est très difficile.
– Ah, oui, c'est vrai, ça.

Worksheets 19a and 19b

Explain to students that they have to get information from each other. Student A and student B have different worksheets and they must not look at the other's worksheet. If necessary, decide who will be student A and who will be student B. All students can then work on Michel's subjects in part **a** whilst you monitor and support them. This will be the time to sort out any problems before students proceed to parts **b**, **c**, and **d**.

ANSWERS FOR ASSESSMENT WORKSHEETS

Worksheet 17
1 a faux, b vrai, c faux, d vrai, e faux, f vrai, g vrai, h vrai.

Worksheet 18
likes - French, technology
dislikes - music, science

Worksheet 20
a English; b Art; c French; d Geography; e History; f Maths; g Music; h Science; i Sport; j Technology.

Worksheet 21
1 Technology; 2 2; 3 English; 4 French; 5 History; 6 1; 7 Sport; 8 Science; 9 Maths; 10 Geography.

Ma ville

Objectives

- to say where you live.
- to describe your home town.
- to understand a brochure describing places in a town.

TEACHING NOTES

STUDENT'S BOOK, page 25

Introduce this new unit by emphasising cross-curricular knowledge.

Display a map of the world. Ask how many countries the students can name where French is one of the languages spoken (e.g. Switzerland, Canada, parts of Africa, e.g. Ivory Coast, The Congo and Zaïre, the Caribbean, Mauritius, etc.). Ask if they have any ideas why these countries should be French speaking.

Look at the pictures on page 25 and ask the students to guess where they are on the map. Why is there variety in the style of housing?

Brainstorm the students for as many French towns as they can name.

Background information

Lots of French towns have places of interest to tourists, especially those founded by the Romans. Towns in the north tend to be more modern, having been rebuilt after the war. Paris is by far the biggest city, with ten million inhabitants. The second biggest city is Lyon, followed by Marseille. France has also created new towns, just as we have created Milton Keynes in England. Cergy-Pointoise serves Paris: as so many people commute from here to work in the city, double-decker trains have to be used.

STUDENT'S BOOK, page 26
Objective 1: to say where you live

Presenting the language

Discuss in English the different forms of the word 'habit' that students have come across, e.g. inhabit, inhabitants, natural habitat, Habitat (the shop). Show them 'habit' on the board or OHP so they can see the connection with the French. Tell the students where you live. Use the class register and ask *Qui habite à . . . ?*, using general areas as opposed to detailed addresses. Now let them say where they live, thus practising *J'habite à . . . .*

Activity 1

Before beginning this activity, the students should look at the photographs and agree

whether each person is male or female. Refresh their memories or introduce them to *filles* and *garçons*. A suggestion to help them remember these words is that *Gary est un garçon* and *Fiona est une fille.*

a
1
– Où habites-tu?
– Bonjour, je m'appelle Nicole. J'habite à Paris.
2
– Où habites-tu?
– Bonjour, je m'appelle Kathy. J'habite à Montréal.
3
– Où habites-tu?
– Bonjour, je m'appelle Qadir. J'habite à Alger.

4
– Où habites-tu?
– Bonjour, je m'appelle Isabelle. J'habite à Fort-de-France.

5
– Où habites-tu?
– Bonjour, je m'appelle Dominique. J'habite à Port Louis.

b
A Bonjour, je m'appelle Kathy. J'habite à Montréal.
B Bonjour, je m'appelle Nicole. J'habite à Paris.
C Bonjour, je m'appelle Dominique. J'habite à Port Louis, île Maurice.
D Bonjour, je m'appelle Qadir. J'habite à Alger.
E Bonjour, je m'appelle Isabelle. J'habite à Fort-de-France.

Differentiation   Distribute pictures of famous people from magazines for students to stick in their books with speech bubbles containing *J'habite à. . . .* Emphasise that the answer does not necessarily have to be correct. In fact, incongruous answers can be amusing.

Give the more able students the task of making a worksheet for those who are still working:

they make a list of characters saying *J'habite à. . . .* on the left side of a page with a list of possible addresses on the right hand side. Other students complete the worksheet.

Activity 2b

Introduce the activity by giving a model answer first, e.g. *Bill Clinton, où habites-tu? J'habite à Washington*. Point out that when talking in the second person, *habites* sounds the same, but the French omit the 's'. Some students can then think of famous people themselves, e.g. *Madonna habite à Hollywood et à Miami et à New York*.

The students pretend to be millionaires and give a press comment, e.g. *J'habite à Malibu*. (Find out which would be the three most popular places to live if they were rich.)

Have a caption competition as homework. See who can think of an original background for *Où habites-tu? J'habite à. . . .*

STUDENT'S BOOK, page 27

Look back at the photographs with the students and go over orally what the words mean first. After completing this written activity, the students say and write correct information about themselves, e.g. *Je m'appelle Stephen. J'habite à Cardiff*. For further practice, add a little light-hearted competiton. Give the students some first names and towns and see if they can match them up, e.g. *Je m'appelle Len Hui. J'habite à Peking* or *Je m'appelle Jurgen. J'habite à Berlin*, etc.

Activity 4

Match the towns with the countries. Port Louis is on the île Maurice and Fort-de-France is on Martinique. Write these, and more examples, on pieces of card. Students work in small

groups. The first group to correctly match them all wins.

Ask the students to translate what Eric Cantona is saying. Can they think of any more famous French people living in the UK? What would these people say?

Patterns of language

Explain that French uses two words for 'you'. Strictly speaking, the *tu* form is for friends and relatives. The more able should be made aware that the polite form, *vous*, would be more appropriate in some of the situations they have come across, e.g. a waiter serving in a café will say *Vous désirez?* when addressing a customer.

STUDENT'S BOOK, pages 28–29
Objective 2: to describe your home town

Presenting the language

Hold up flashcards of the cognates and give alternative answers in the first instance, e.g.

C'est un hôpital où un cinéma? Practise until the students can actively say what all the places are. Explain that *il y a. . .* can mean both 'there is' or 'there are'. Describe where you live to the class, e.g. *J'habite à Hull. Dans ma ville, il y a un hôpital à Anlaby Road. Il y a une discothèque.*

Activity 1

Students can make multiple choice quizzes for their partners. They draw a symbol of a hospital then write, for example **a** *C'est un hôpital?* **b** *C'est un marché?* **c** *C'est un discothèque?*

Activity 2

With the exceptions of *théâtre* and *centre sportif*, the students will probably need support with these words. Miming and giving examples of names, e.g. shops near the school, will help students to guess the meaning.

1 Dans ma ville, il y a une gare.
2 Dans ma ville, il y a un musée.
3 Dans ma ville, il y a des magasins.
4 Dans ma ville, il y a un centre sportif.
5 Dans ma ville, il y a un théâtre.
6 Dans ma ville, il y a une piscine.
7 Dans ma ville, il y a un stade.

Ask the students to bring in postcards (and provide some yourself) with any of these words on. Practise the pronunciation in pairs; one partner holds the cards in a fan shape and the other partner has to say the words to gain the card until they are all gone.

Activity 3

Students can repeat all the phrases at first and then they repeat only the phrases of places in their town. They could also listen to the place on tape and say *oui* or *non*, depending on whether or not the place is in their town.

– Il y a un cinéma.
– Il y a une piscine.
– Il y a une discothèque.
– Il y a un théâtre.
– Il y a un marché.
– Il y a un musée.

– Il y a une cathédrale.
– Il y a des magasins.
– Il y a une poste.
– Il y a un stade.
– Il y a un hypermarché.
– Il y un centre sportif.
– Il y a un hôpital.
– Il y a une gare.

Activity 4

Practise the question *Qu'est-ce qu'il y a dans la ville?* orally lots of times before letting the students read it. Students then ask the question in different styles, e.g. as if they were a young child or an impatient tourist in 'Fawlty Towers'. Ask students to suggest contexts in which they would find the question relevant.

Activity 5

The students could choose another town in the locality and describe it without naming the town. Their partner then has to guess which town it is. Agree beforehand which towns would be allowed! For students who need further reinforcement, pretend to be a tourist guide on a bus. Some students sit in a line, pretending to be tourists. One can ask *Qu'est-ce qu'il y a dans la ville?* Another student stands at the front with a microphone. A third student stands at the side with flashcards. As the 'guide' mentions the place, the person with the flashcards selects the right card and then goes down the side as if they are driving past.

Activity 6

After the students have put the words they know into alphabetical order, develop this into a Yellow Pages book (*les Pages Jaunes*). Students find the phone numbers of the places from a genuine Yellow Pages and they then make a simple version as if making it for a French visitor to the town. Print on yellow paper from the computer.

STUDENT'S BOOK, page 30
Objective 3: to understand a brochure describing places in a town

Activity 1

Remind the students that this activity is based on GCSE reading questions, the sort they would find in the basic reading tests. Emphasise that they do not have to understand every word. Read through the two advertisements first with the class, then read the questions carefully before returning to the adverts.

For students who lack confidence, part **b** could be completed orally before they return to do it individually at a later stage. The more able students could invent their own advertisements

---

based on these, changing the names of the towns and the attractions for visitors. For homework, they could illustrate their work or find pictures in holiday brochures.

Activity 2

Students can pretend they are taking part in the 'conveyor-belt game' on the 'Generation Game'. Every place you mention, you can visit on your grand tour game!

For more revision on the place names, play the 'telepathy game'. A volunteer describes a scene from a postcard, e.g. *Il y a une cathédrale et un marché*, etc. Four other volunteers draw. The picture most closely matching the postcard wins.

Activity 3

After completing this task, consolidate with more practice. Using pieces of card, stick a picture on one side of each. Hang the cards from the ceiling – alarms permitting!

Students role-play the scene, e.g. an over-worked boss on a business trip dictates to his/her secretary what to write down on a postcard.

Students give a list on the OHP of tourist towns they have visited. They copy down attractions on the left hand side of their paper. They choose two towns and make a column for each town. They then give points out of five for each attraction. Which is voted best town?

	Londres	Chester
un marché	**	*
une discothèque	***	*
un musée	***	***

Further ideas for revision: take slides of the students' home town. Show the slides and ask what the places are. Make an audio cassette recording of the pupils saying what the places are and synchronise this to make a slideshow presentation.

Practise *Qu'est-ce qu'il y a dans la ville?* This time, video the students in front of the screen whilst the slides are being shown and ask them to introduce one place at a time on the screen.

Differentiation   Giving definitions of words is an invaluable linguistic skill. If you do not actively know a word, can you describe or mime it? The students who may be taking the GCSE examination could complete a crossword which you give them, helping them if necessary with mime, e.g. *Tu regardes un film ici/Tu danses ici/Tu joues au squash ici*, etc.

STUDENT'S BOOK, page 31

Le sommaire

Play 'Blockbuster' as a revision game. Write initials in permanent ink on separate pieces of paper. When students answer, they can colour over their 'inital' in non-permanent ink. The first team to get four in a row wins. Definitions can be given in English or French depending on ability.

C – tu regardes un film ici/Odeon
P – nager (mime it)
T – give students the name of a local theatre
D – tu danses ici
M – tu regardes
M – Harrods, Harvey Nicholls, etc.

G – tu prends le train
M – bananes/oranges (mime stallholder)
C – Quasimodo habite ici
S – Wembley
P – tu envoies une lettre où carte postale
H – il y a un. . . à Calais pour les touristes anglais
H – give students the name of a local hospital
CS – tu joues au squash/badminton ici
V – Lincoln, c'est une. . .
OHT – where do you live?
J'H – I live
DMV – in my town

TRANSITION TO GCSE

This unit forms a very sound basis for GCSE. In addition, students will need to:

- state the location of where they live.
  C'est dans le nord/le sud/l'est/l'ouest.
- describe their town (village).
  C'est un petit village.
  C'est une grande ville industrielle.

Check your GCSE syllabus to see which adjectives and additional places students will need to learn. Again, concentrate firstly on the words to describe their own town (village). Others are taught for receptive purposes only.

This would be a good opportunity to teach students a bit more about France. Select well-known French towns and make students aware of their geographical position in France. Copy a map of France onto an OHT. Describe a town. Students come to the OHT and point to the town on the map, etc.

C'est une ville touristique dans le sud de la France.

Further practice on this topic can be found in **Vital 2**, *Unité 1.*

USE OF ASSESSMENT WORKSHEETS

Worksheet 24

Task A: Students are asked to colour in the drawings of the places they hear on the recording. If colours are not available, the students can either tick the appropriate drawing or shade them in pen or pencil.

– Alors, on commence. Nous sommes maintenant à la gare SNCF. Nous allons d'abord au marché qui se trouve tout près de la gare. Bon. Comme vous le voyez, il y a des magasins à côté du marché et voici la poste. On va maintenant à la cathédrale et vous avez une heure pour visiter la cathédrale et le musée. Après avoir visité la cathédrale on va visiter le théâtre. Après, on va visiter le stade et la piscine. Alors, on se retrouve ici dans une heure, c'est-à-dire à 14 heures.

Worksheet 25

– J'habite dans une petite ville dans le nord de la France. Dans ma ville, il y une grande place avec beaucoup de magasins. Tous les jeudis, il y a aussi un marché. Pour les jeunes, il y a un stade où on peut faire tous les sports. On peut aussi nager à la piscine municipale. Il y a un cinéma, mais il n'y a pas de théâtre. Pour les touristes, il y a un musée avec une exposition sur l'histoire de la ville.

Worksheet 26

The drawings are on the worksheet only as a prompt for students. They do not need to include all the places in their description.

ANSWERS FOR ASSESSMENT WORKSHEETS

Worksheet 24
station, market, shops, post office, cathedral, museum, theatre, stadium, swimming pool

Worksheet 25
1 shops, museum, stadium, market, swimming pool, cinema

Worksheet 28
1 a town, b market, c tennis, football, swim
2 a iii and iv, b ii and iii, c ii and iii

Le bon chemin

UNIT 5

Objectives

- to ask for directions.
- to understand and give directions.
- to write a set of directions.

TEACHING NOTES

STUDENT'S BOOK, page 32

Brainstorm in English the language they feel they would need to survive were they to get lost in France. Brainstorm realistic situations in which students think they may be asked for directions in French. Point out that in their working life, they may come across French-speaking people on placement in the UK.

STUDENT'S BOOK, page 33
Objective 1: to ask for directions

Presenting the language

Teach/revise the names of the five places illustrated here, to use the language for directions in a realistic context. See Teacher's Book, Unit 4, for ideas on presentation of places.

Explain again to students that they only need to add *s'il vous plaît* (in a questioning tone) to the name of the place they are trying to get to. Give them plenty of practice with this using flashcards 27–40.

Activity 1

a
1 Monsieur, la gare, s'il vous plaît.
2 Madame, le cinéma, s'il vous plaît.
3 Monsieur, la discothèque, s'il vous plaît.
4 Excusez-moi, le stade, s'il vous plaît.
5 Madame, la poste, s'il vous plaît.

If they need further practice with this, ask them to repeat only the names of the places, as if they were checking that they had heard properly.

This is also an excellent communication skill.

b
1 La poste, s'il vous plaît?
2 Le cinéma, s'il vous plaît?
3 Le stade, s'il vous plaît?
4 La discothèque, s'il vous plaît?
5 La gare, s'il vous plaît?

Differentiation More able students could extend this activity by checking comprehension (see Activity 1). This can be quite an entertaining exercise if the person checking comprehension pretends to have misheard, e.g.

– *La gare, s'il vous plaît?*
– *Le cinema?*
– *Non, la gare, s'il vous plaît?*
– *La poste?*

STUDENT'S BOOK, pages 34–35
Objective 2: to understand and give directions

Presenting the language

Introduce the three words/expressions *gauche*, *tout droit* and *droite* by miming as an air steward/stewardess in the safety demonstrations. Draw arrows on the board. Students point out the correct one when you say *gauche* or *droite*. Have two volunteers at the board with chalk or markers. Another volunteer shouts a direction for those at the board to draw. The first person to draw the arrow stays at the board to be challenged!

Practise the three directions with gimmicks such as a toy remote controlled car. The first student to say a direction correctly has a turn steering the car according to directions given by the other students.

The French word *gauche* means clumsy or socially inept in English, whereas *adroit* means skilful.

Activity 1

a

1 Vous tournez à gauche.
2 Vous tournez à droite.
3 Vous allez tout droit.
4 Vous allez tout droit et vous tournez à gauche.

b
1
– Vous allez à la gare!
– La gare?
– Oui, la gare. Vous prenez la deuxième rue à gauche.
– La deuxième rue à gauche? O.K!
2
– Vous allez à la poste!
– Oui, la poste. Vous prenez la première rue à droite.
3
– Vous allez au cinéma!
– Oui, le cinéma. Vous prenez la troisième rue à gauche.

Extend this activity with further role-play.

Prepare an observation puzzle for them on the OHP. Draw four boxes. In the boxes draw buildings with the names they already know in French. Describe the boxes whilst the students can still see them, e.g. *La poste est à gauche. L'hôtel est à droite.*

Ask questions in French while they can still see, e.g. *Où est l'hôtel, dessin 1?*, etc.

Describe a picture and the students say which number it is. Have an OHP prepared with silhouettes of the pictures. Students then describe the pictures in French. Students then describe to volunteers who make up four new pictures on a new OHP.

Activity 2

For further practice, students could listen again after completing the activities, but this time they draw symbols for buildings and directions. Read back the 'shorthand' (symbols) in French.

Play charades; one team mimes, for example, 'Where is the station?', with directions, while another team 'narrates' in French.

Give the class a quiz. Ask the following questions in English. Students write *gauche* or *droite* accordingly:

1 On which side of the road do cars drive in France? (*droite*)
2 Which side of the page do English people look at first? (*gauche*)
3 On a keyboard, which side is 'q' on? (*gauche*)
4 Which way do you look first when crossing the road in France? (*droite*)
5 Which arm did Napoleon lose? (*droite*)

Before starting activity 3, explain the word *première*, using dates, e.g. *1 mai, 1 septembre, 1 décembre*. Ask the students if they can work out premier from 'premier league' or a film premier. Explain *deuxième* and *troisième*.

Activity 3

– Madame, la gare, s'il vous plaît.
– Vous prenez la deuxième rue à gauche.
– Monsieur, la poste, s'il vous plaît.
– Vous prenez la première rue à droite.
– Madame, les magasins, s'il vous plaît.
– Vous prenez la troisième rue à droite.
– Monsieur, le cinéma, s'il vous plaît.
– Vous prenez la deuxième rue à droite.
– Madame, le stade, s'il vous plaît.
– Vous prenez la troisième rue à gauche.

Activity 4

Ask the students for further ideas for working the dialogue, if you think this is necessary.

a & b

– Excusez-moi, la gare s'il vous plaît?
– La gare? Vous prenez la première rue à droite.
– Merci, monsieur.

Students could practise this and perform the role-play for the rest of the class.

d

1
– La poste, c'est la première rue à droite?
– Oui, la première rue à droite.
2
– La gare, c'est la deuxième rue à gauche?
3
– La discothèque, c'est la première rue à gauche?
4
– Le cinéma, c'est la troisième rue à droite?

STUDENT'S BOOK, page 36
Objective 3: to write a set of directions

Activity 1

a

1 Vous prenez la première rue à gauche. La gare.
2 Vous prenez la troisième rue à droite.
3 Vous prenez la deuxième rue à gauche.
4 Vous allez tout droit.
5 Vous prenez la première rue à droite.

Activity 2

More able students could write directions to other places, too.

Differentiation For more able students, photocopy a map of the area surrounding the school. Students write directions to places which they have translated into French, e.g. *La gare? Allez tout droit. Prenez la deuxième rue à gauche*, etc.

For further practice at writing directions, make up and give out photocopies of a map which has more than one or two of each of the places they know, e.g. two discos. Agree a starting point. Each student writes notes on paper, giving directions where to meet. See how many end up at the same place.

TRANSITION TO GCSE

Check your GCSE syllabus for any additional places you may need to teach. If you are working chronologically through **French Plus**, you will already have covered this additional vocabulary in Unit 4.

In addition to the directions taught in Unit 5, students will need to:

● ask (state) if there is a place nearby.
Il y a . . . près d'ici?

● state if a place is near/a long way off.
C'est près d'ici.
C'est loin.

Check your GCSE syllabus to see if students need also to know some prepositions.

Practise prepositions by placing flashcards of buildings in appropriate places on the wall. Describe the position of the flashcards, e.g. *L'hôtel est en face de la gare*. Students say whether the statement is true or false. Say similar statements based on pictures of buildings placed on the OHP. Students repeat the correct statements and correct the incorrect statements.

Finally, volunteer students can come to the OHP and make a statement about the position of a building. The rest of the class accepts or corrects the statements.

Further practice on this topic can be found in **Vital 1**, *Unité 5*.

USE OF ASSESSMENT WORKSHEETS

Worksheet 32

Dialogue 1
– Excusez-moi, madame. Où est la cathédrale, s'il vous plaît?
– La cathédrale. . . vous allez à droite.
– A droite?
– Oui, monsieur.
– Merci, madame. Au revoir.
– Au revoir, monsieur.

Dialogue 2
– Excusez-moi. Où sont les magasins, s'il vous plaît?
– Les magasins . . . vous allez à gauche, monsieur.
– A gauche?
– Oui.
– Merci. Au revoir.
– Au revoir, monsieur.

Dialogue 3
– Excusez-moi, madame. Où est la poste, s'il vous plaît?
– La poste . . . vous prenez la troisième rue à gauche.
– La troisième rue à gauche?
– Oui.
– Merci, madame. Au revoir.
– Au revoir.

Dialogue 4
– Excusez-moi, monsieur. Le stade, s'il vous plaît?
– Le stade. . . vous prenez la première rue à droite.
– La première rue à droite?
– Oui.
– Merci, monsieur. Au revoir.
– Au revoir.

Worksheet 33

1

Dialogue A
– Excusez-moi, monsieur. La gare, s'il vous plaît?
– La gare. . . vous allez tout droit, madame.
– Tout droit.
– Oui, vous allez tout droit et vous prenez la première rue à droite.
– Tout droit et la première rue à droite.
– Oui, madame.
– Merci, monsieur. Au revoir.
– Au revoir, madame.

Dialogue B
– Excusez-moi, madame. Où est l'hôpital, s'il vous plaît?
– L'hôpital. . . vous allez tout droit, monsieur.
– Tout droit.
– Oui, vous allez tout droit et vous prenez la deuxième rue à gauche.
– Tout droit et la deuxième rue à gauche.
– Oui, monsieur.
– Merci, madame. Au revoir.
– Au revoir, monsieur.

Activity 2
– Excusez-moi, monsieur. Le stade, s'il vous plaît?
– Le stade. . . vous prenez la première rue à droite, monsieur.
– La première rue à droite.
– Oui, vous prenez la première rue à droite et la deuxième rue à gauche.
– La première rue à droite et la deuxième rue à gauche.
– Oui, monsieur.
– Merci, monsieur. Au revoir.
– Au revoir.

Worksheet 34
Discuss the symbols with your students so that they are clear what they have to do before they start the role-play.

ANSWERS FOR ASSESSMENT WORKSHEETS

Worksheet 32
1b, 2c, 3c, 4c

Worksheet 37
a2, b3, c5, d6, e1, f4

Temps libre

Objectives

- to talk about your interests and activities.
- to express an opinion about activities.
- to write about your favourite interests and activities.

TEACHING NOTES

STUDENT'S BOOK, page 38

Ask the students to look at the collage of photographs and see if they all agree what the freetime activities depicted are.

Discuss in English how they spend their free time. Do they feel they have enough free time after school and homework? How do they spend time at weekends and in their holidays?

How much of an influence does the weather have on their time outside school? Would they have different interests if they lived in the Alps or Corsica or Mauritius?

How important is it to have money? Can one have a hobby or interest without spending anything?

Ask them if they feel it is important to have an interest outside school or work.

Background information

Football is the most popular sport in France. Well-known French footballers in the UK include Eric Cantona and David Ginola. The French Cup Final and many international games are played at the Parc des Princes stadium in Paris. There are over 20,000 football clubs in France.

The French Rugby Union team is considered to be one of the most exciting teams to watch, and Rugby League is gaining a foothold because of Paris St. Germain's introduction into the European Super League.

Cycling is also very poular in France and the Tour de France is one of the world's best-known cycle races. It is usually held in July and is relayed by television to millions of viewers worldwide.

Other poular sports in France include tennis, skiing and basketball. Popular spectator sports are horse-racing, motor racing, and boxing.

Cinema is a very popular pastime in France and despite the advent of the video, the French film industry continues to thrive. TV is also a popular leisure time activity; France has six TV channels to choose from.

STUDENT'S BOOK, pages 39–40
Objective 1: to talk about your interests and activities

Presenting the language

Use flashcards 45–52, which show various interests and activities. Hold them and say what they all are, e.g. *Je joue avec l'ordinateur; je joue au football; je regarde la télé; je fais du* *vélo*, etc. Take care to group the activities according to the three verbs. Repeat the French, this time sticking the cards in the three groups onto the board. See if the students heard the verbs, then write *je joue, je regarde* and *je fais* above each group of cards. Turn the cards over and stick them so that the students see only the silhouettes. The student then says the verb they can see plus the activity depicted by the silhouette. When they can do that, wipe off the verb so that the students just have the silhouettes as a prompt for both the verbs and the nouns. Now practise the question *Qu'est-ce que tu fais le week-end?*, pointing to a silhouette. The students practise the question and answers until they are confident.

Activity 1

If students need further repetition practice, ask them to repeat only the pastimes that they like.

a, b & c

– Qu'est-ce que tu fais le week-end, Marc?
– Euh, je joue au football, je joue avec l'ordinateur et je fais du vélo.
– Qu'est-ce que tu fais le week-end, Julie?
– Je fais les magasins, je regarde la télé et je fais du vélo.

For the final part of the activity, some students may need you to provide them with a worksheet which lists the missing words.

Differentiation   The more able students can translate the words in the speech bubbles and invent their own 'cartoons'. The less able can copy carefully.

For further practice, the students 'act out' the photograph. It is also fun to take photographs of them asking the question *Qu'est-ce que tu fais le week-end?* When the photographs are developed, stick the speech bubbles on them.

When students feel comfortable with the question *Qu'est-ce que tu fais le week-end?*, introduce the fourth verb, *je vais. . . .* The students ask the teacher the question; the teacher replies *Je vais à Manchester*, or any local town. Check in English that the students have guessed the meaning of *Je vais. . . .*

Bring in a box of visual aids such as a bus ticket for *Je vais en ville*, a glittering accessory for *Je vais en discothèque*, a cup for *Je vais au café*, a diary with phone numbers for *Je vais chez les copains*, a pair of swimming trunks for *Je vais à la piscine*, a card cut out of a fish for *Je vais à la pêche* and a pair of glasses for *Je vais au cinéma*.

The teacher says one of the places, e.g. *Je vais à la pêche* and a volunteer picks out the appropriate visual aid. Practise further by asking more able students to say the place while the less able find the visual aid.

Activity 2

– Je vais à la pêche.   – Je vais en discothèque.
– Je vais en ville.   – Je vais chez les copains.
– Je vais au café.   – Je vais au cinéma.
– Je vais à la piscine.

Activity 3

Practise this activity further by making an audio recording of the correct dialogue. Play 'speakquence'; one student says the verb, the other student the place.

b

– Qu'est-ce que tu fais le week-end?
– Je vais au café, je vais en discothèque et je vais à la pêche.

Activity 4

Further ways of acting out the dialogue could be elicited from the students. They might include pretending to be famous or rich people!

Patterns of language

Explain that the words *joue, regarde, fais* and *vais* are verbs and that *je* means 'I' and *tu* means 'you', when talking to a friend, relative or young person.

STUDENT'S BOOK, page 41
Objective 2: to express an opinion about activities

Presenting the language

Revise, or introduce *j'aime*. Put some posters or photographs of famous people or places around the room. Be dramatic (when walking round the room) to illustrate, e.g. *J'aime Peter Andre*, said with a sigh and a hand on heart,

---

then *Je n'aime pas. . .* , said with thumbs down and a look of disgust. Students point to the posters and say *J'aime. . .* or *Je n'aime pas. . . .*

Now introduce the activites. Put the flashcards used previously on the board in four groups as the pupils say them (they say, for example, *la piscine*). When the nouns are in the four groups, write the verbs at the top of each group in a colour, e.g. green. In the middle of the board write *j'aime* in red, surrounded by a heart shape.

Explain that to make sentences they need a red (*j'aime*), a green (*aller*) and a white chalk/black marker word (*au cinéma*). Divide the class into groups and distribute a set of word cards to each group – words in red, green and black. See which group can order the cards correctly first.

Activity 1

a

– Qu' est-ce que tu aimes faire?
– J'aime aller au cinéma.
   J'aime aller en discothèque.
   J'aime aller au café.
   J'aime aller chez les copains.
   J'aime aller à la piscine.
   J'aime aller à la pêche.

– Qu'est-ce que tu aimes faire?
– J'aime regarder la télé.
   J'aime jouer au foot.
   J'aime jouer avec l'ordinateur.
   J'aime faire du vélo.
   J'aime faire les magasins.

If the pupils need further practice with this, use another selective technique, e.g. *Notez les activités que vous aimez faire le week-end.*

Activity 2

When conducting a survey, decide beforehand who will be moving and who will remain seated! Any talking in English is forbidden! Results could be illustrated in a number of ways, i.e. graphs, bar charts, pie charts, collage, etc.

Differentiation   More able students who finish early could do a further list where they write out what they think their partner's favourite pastimes are. The two lists could then be compared!

STUDENT'S BOOK, page 42
Objective 3: to write about your favourite interests and activities

Activity 1

– Qu'est-ce que tu aimes faire, Julie?
– J'aime aller au café.
   J'aime aller à la piscine.
   J'aime jouer avec l'ordinateur.
   J'aime faire les magasins.
   J'aime regarder la télé.
– Qu'est-ce que tu aimes faire, Marc?
– J'aime aller à la pêche.
   J'aime aller chez les copains.
   J'aime jouer au foot.
   J'aime jouer avec l'ordinateur.
   J'aime regarder la télé.
– Qu'est-ce que tu aimes faire, Sandrine?
– J'aime aller en discothèque.
   J'aime aller en ville.
   J'aime faire du vélo.
   J'aime faire les magasins.
   J'aime regarder la télé.

Differentiation   Have some photocopies of the grid ready for those who find it difficult or demotivating to copy. While more able students are copying the grid, explain the activity again to the less able and give examples of what they might hear and what they should do. Some students may feel more confident if you read through all the activities with them before playing the tape.

Activity 2

For those students who feel discouraged by a lot of text, enlarge the screens on a photocopier. Next to each screen have a picture of a person or a name, as well as the letter. Ask some questions in English such as:

1 Who likes watching television?
2 Who likes going to the cinema?

3 Who likes cycling?
4 Who likes fishing?
5 What does A like doing?

The more able students who do not have photographs on their sheet can be asked who are more likely to be boys or girls. Point out that these types of questions can be found in the GCSE reading tests.

For the second part of the activity, if it is not possible to use word-processors, make an attractive display of 'mock' computer screens, colouring over their text in green.

For further practice, students note down their likes and dislikes on paper with their initials on. They fold them up and hand them in. See whose notes are similar and whether or not they are friends!

For further practice, read a mock 'starsign' book in French. Ask if the statements are *vrai ou faux*:

1 Bélier (21 mars – 20 avril) Tu aimes aller au cinéma.
2 Taureau (21 avril – 21 mai) Tu aimes faire du vélo.
3 Gémeaux (22 mai – 21 juin) Tu aimes aller chez les copains.

4 Cancer (22 juin – 22 juillet) Tu aimes regarder la télé.
5 Lion (23 juillet – 22 août) Tu aimes aller en discothèque.
6 Vierge (23 août – 22 septembre) Tu aimes aller au café.
7 Balance (23 septembre – 22 octobre) Tu aimes aller en ville.
8 Scorpion (23 octobre – 21 novembre) Tu aimes aller faire les magasins.
9 Sagittaire (22 novembre – 20 décembre) Tu aimes jouer au football.
10 Capricorne (21 décembre – 19 janvier) Tu aimes jouer avec l'ordinateur.
11 Verseau (20 janvier – 19 février) Tu aimes aller à la pêche.
12 Poissons (20 février – 20 mars) Tu aimes aller à la piscine.

As a consolidation exercise, the students choose twelve people to match to each of the activities of the unit. They then write this up in twelve sentences, e.g. *Eddie aime faire les magasins*, etc. This work could be illustrated for display with photos of the students/pictures of the activities, etc.

TRANSITION TO GCSE

This unit covers a large amount of the language needed for GCSE. In particular, students will benefit from the ability to express an opinion; language which is taught in Unit 6, e.g. *J'aime faire du vélo/Je n'aime pas aller en ville.*

The ability to express an opinion is a requirement for a grade C at GCSE. If your students can produce an opinion, it will improve their overall grade.

In addition, students' grades at GCSE will be improved if they can state one activity which they have done in the past. The grammatical construction of the perfect tense does not need

to be explained. Students can learn their chosen phrase as a set phrase.

The list of phrases below offers students a selection of very simple references to past activities:

J'ai joué au foot (avec l'ordinateur).
J'ai été au cinéma (au café) (chez les copains) (à la piscine).
J'ai fait les magasins (du vélo).

Students should choose one phrase from this list and learn it as a response to *Qu'est-ce que tu as fait, le week-end dernier?*

Further practice on this topic can be found in **Vital 1**, *Unité 8* and *Unité 13*.

USE OF ASSESSMENT WORKSHEETS

Worksheet 40

1

Dialogue 1
– Qu'est ce-que tu aimes faire?
– J'aime regarder la télé, j'aime faire les magasins et j'aime aller en discothèque.

Dialogue 2
– Qu'est ce-que tu aimes faire?
– J'aime aller à la piscine, j'aime aller au cinéma et j'aime jouer avec l'ordinateur.

Dialogue 3
– Qu'est ce-que tu aimes faire?
– Moi, j'aime faire du vélo, j'aime jouer au football et j'aime aller à la pêche.

2

– Salut! Je m'appelle Paul. J'ai 15 ans. J'aime faire du vélo, j'aime aller à la piscine et j'aime regarder la télé.

Worksheet 41

1

1 Bonjour. Je m'appelle Alexandre. J'ai 13 ans. Le samedi, je fais les magasins. J'aime aller en ville.
2 Bonjour. Je m'appelle Julie. Le samedi, je vais de temps en temps au cinéma. Le dimanche, je regarde la télé. J'aime regarder la télé.
3 Je m'appelle Nicolas. Le samedi, je joue au football. Le dimanche, je vais chez mes copains. J'aime aller chez les copains.
4 Salut! Je m'appelle Céline. Le samedi matin, je joue avec l'ordinateur. Le dimanche, je fais souvent du vélo. J'aime faire du vélo.
5 Salut! Je m'appelle Thomas. Le samedi, je vais à la piscine. Le dimanche, je vais souvent à la pêche. J'aime beaucoup aller à la pêche.

Worksheets 41 and 42

On both worksheets, activity 2 is not an assessed activity.

Worksheet 42

1

– Moi, j'aime faire les magasins, j'aime aller à la piscine et j'aime jouer avec l'ordinateur.
– Moi, j'aime aller chez les copains, j'aime aller au café et j'aime regarder la télé.
– Moi, j'aime regarder la télé, j'aime faire du vélo et j'aime aller au cinéma.
– Moi, j'aime aller chez les copains, j'aime jouer au football et j'aime regarder la télé.
– Moi, j'aime aller au café, j'aime aller chez les copains et j'aime faire les magasins.
– Moi, j'aime jouer au football, j'aime regarder la télé et j'aime aller chez les copains.
– Moi, j'aime aller au cinéma, j'aime faire les magasins et j'aime aller chez les copains.

Worksheets 44 and 45

Worksheet 44, which tests discrete phrases, acts as preparation for Worksheet 45 where students are tested on these phrases within short texts. Students must complete Worksheet 45 to achieve the outcome.

Worksheet 46

In task B, students need only to adapt the incorrect phrases from task A. Explain to students that they will need only to copy the phrase and change some of the words. This is not an assessed task.

ANSWERS FOR ASSESSMENT WORKSHEETS

Worksheet 40
1 1 Anne; 2 Claudette; 3 Nicole.
2 Paul: cycling, swimming, television.

Worksheet 41
1 Alexandre: shopping, going to town. Julie: cinema, television. Nicolas: football, visiting friends.
Céline: computers, cycling. Thomas: swimming, fishing.

Worksheet 42
shopping 1 1 1	swimming 1
cycling 1	fishing
cinema 1 1	football 1 1
visiting friends 1 1 1 1 1	computer 1
café 1 1	television 1 1 1 1

Worksheet 44
1 a 3; b 10; c 1; d 4; e 6; f 8; g 7; h 2.

Worksheet 45
1 1c; 3a; 4b.
2 I'm called Jean-Paul. I'm 13. At the weekend I play on the computer, I go to town, I watch television and I go to the cinema. I like cycling and I like going to the swimming-pool.

Worksheet 46
1 a V; b V; c F; d F; e V; f V; g F; h F.
2 Julie aime aller à la piscine. Matthieu aime faire les magasins. Thomas aime faire du vélo. Marc aime regarder la télé.

Le temps

Objectives

- to describe what the weather is like today.
- to describe weather in different seasons.
- to write about the weather where you are.

TEACHING NOTES

STUDENT'S BOOK, page 44

Discuss the objectives with the students. Brainstorm the class for as many descriptions of the weather as they can think of. Mention the fact that the weather is often a good topic of conversation with strangers and discuss clichés of climate. Is it really always raining in England? Point out that while the north of France has very similar seasons to the UK, the seasons in the midi are more marked with much hotter and drier summers.

Background information

Point out to pupils (using a map of western Europe or France and her neighbours) that France is a large country in relation to the UK and it, therefore, has a more varied climate depending on which part of France you are in. Explain that it is the climate in the north of France that is most like UK weather and that there is said to be a marked difference in the climate south of the Loire. Discuss the climate in francophone countries and the contrast between, e.g. Canada and Martinique.

STUDENT'S BOOK, pages 45–46
Objective 1: to describe what the weather is like today

Presenting the language

Present the weather vocabulary in groups of two or three expressions at a time. Use realia wherever possible to lend authenticity to the presentation (umbrella for *il pleut*, sunglasses for *il fait du soleil*, etc.). Reinforce new vocabulary actively by, for example, getting students to mime a weather expression.

Use games to reinforce the vocabulary. Play *'Morpion'* by drawing a grid on the OHP and putting a weather symbol in each square. In teams, students have to describe the weather to get their nought or cross in the square.

Bring in some newspapers and glossy magazines. Students work through them in pairs, taking turns to describe any weather pictures they find.

Activity 1

Prepare students for this activity by focussing on France. See how many French towns they can name. Discuss the effect of landscape on climate (e.g. the Alps, sea, lowland, etc.). Practise the pronunciation of the towns (Le Havre, Boulogne, Paris, Grenoble, Chamonix, Nice, Calais, Strasbourg, Cannes, Lyon, Marseille) before playing the tape.

- Paris
- Cannes
- Nice
- Le Havre
- Boulogne
- Strasbourg
- Chamonix
- Lyon
- Grenoble
- Calais
- Marseille

Activity 2

1 A Marseille, il fait chaud.
2 A Calais, il pleut.
3 A Lyon, il fait beau.
4 A Strasbourg, il neige.
5 A Cannes, il fait du soleil.

Activity 3

– Il fait du brouillard.
– Il pleut.
– Il fait beau.
– Il fait froid.
– Il neige.
– Il fait du vent.

– Il pleut.
– Il neige.
– Il fait du soleil.
– Il fait beau.
– Il fait chaud.

Differentiation   Less able students may need further repetition practice. If this is the case, allow them to listen to the tape again, repeating all the expressions, in a small group or through the headphones. Meanwhile, more able pupils could complete a written exercise. From a list of expressions, written at random on the OHP, students look at the symbols next to the towns on the map and write a sentence for each, e.g. *A Boulougne, il pleut*. They could then draw a symbol to illustrate each sentence.

Activity 4

If possible, bring in pictures/brochures which illustrate each of these activities. Ask students to describe the weather on each picture. Follow this up by asking, e.g. *Et c'est le temps idéal pour faire du ski?* Try to reach a consensus on what is the ideal/nightmare weather for each of the activities, before allowing the students to begin writing. Any students with literacy difficulties could draw symbols on the grid.

Activity 5

A Le ski: temps idéal – il neige; temps pas idéal – il fait chaud.
B La voile: temps idéal – il fait du vent; temps pas idéal – il fait du brouillard.
C La pêche: temps idéal – il fait beau; temps pas idéal – il pleut.
D Le patinage: temps idéal – il fait froid; temps pas idéal – il fait chaud.

Activity 6

Before beginning this activity, introduce *Quel temps fait-il?* Use mime to ask what the weather is like today. Use the weather map on page 45 or newspaper weather reports to give students plenty of practice with this. It is especially motivating for students if you bring in French national weather reports. Get them to underline the key words only and then practise the dialogue, e.g. *Quel temps fait-il à Boulogne?*, etc.

Hold a *météo* quiz with two teams and two sets of flashcards. Each team member has to hold up a flashcard and ask *Quel temps fait-il?* A member of the other team describes the weather.

Patterns of language

Point out that most of the expressions for weather begin with *il fait. . .* (this verb precedes *beau, mauvais, chaud, froid, du soleil, du brouillard, du vent*), the exceptions being *il pleut* and *il neige*. The students could make their own flow chart from this information.

STUDENT'S BOOK, page 47
Objective 2: to describe weather in different seasons

Presentation of language

Introduce the seasons by dividing an OHT into four parts. Place an overlay on it showing the months. Put cut-outs of trees, flowers, etc. into each box as you describe the seasons. Get the students to put the right cut-outs into the right season. When students are ready, move on to the activities.

Activity 1

– Il fait du soleil. . . en été.
– Il fait du vent. . .
– Il fait du brouillard. . .
– Il neige. . .
– Il fait chaud. . .
– Il fait beau. . .
– Il fait froid. . .
– Il pleut. . .

Activity 2

– A Marseille, il fait chaud.
– A Grenoble, il fait froid.
– A Boulogne, il pleut.
– A Cannes, il fait du soleil.
– A Strasbourg, il neige.
– A Paris, il fait beau.
– A Calais, il fait du brouillard.
– A Lyon, il fait du vent.

You could extend this activity by asking students to audition to be a weather forecaster. They read aloud descriptions of the weather in their town in the different seasons, e.g. *A Manchester en été, il fait chaud et il fait du soleil.*

Activity 3

Work this exercise orally with the class before allowing them to match up the sentences.

Differentiation More able students could extend this activity by adding an extra weather expression to each of the sentences, e.g. *Au printemps, il fait du vent et il pleut.*

Activity 4

Read the extract with the students and check for comprehension. Stress that they do not have to understand every word.

STUDENT'S BOOK, page 48
Objective 3: to write about the weather where you are

Before beginning the activities, brainstorm different holiday destinations and write them up on the OHP/board. Students describe the weather in each of the places and you put each place into one of two lists: *Il fait chaud/Il fait froid*. Students could write two further lists, *Il pleut/Il fait du soleil*, and categorise each of the places accordingly.

Activity 1

Read through the postcard with the class to check comprehension.

Divide the class into two halves. Ask one half of the class to write as many expressions as they

can think of for the first postcard in two minutes, while the other half writes as many as they can think of for the second postcard. After the time is up, students volunteer expressions, which you put on the OHP/board (in two lists). They should then have all the weather information they need to write the card of their choice.

As a homework activity, let students choose a holiday destination from brochures you have brought in advertising francophone countries (e.g. Quebec, Martinique, Morocco, etc). Ask them to write you a postcard, describing the weather where they are.

TRANSITION TO GCSE

This unit forms a sound basis for the requirements of GCSE. The major weather phrases are taught together with the seasons. Students will, in addition, need to recognise and understand these phrases in weather forecasts where they will appear in a future tense. The most common form of the future tense which students will need to understand is *Il va faire beau/Il va pleuvoir*, etc.

Students should be given practice in linking weather forecasts with proposed activities, e.g.

A: *Qu'est-ce qu'on fait?*
B: *Demain, il va pleuvoir. On va au cinéma.*

As students' comprehension will often be tested through the use of symbols, make sure that students easily recognise standard symbols from weather maps. Copy the symbols onto an OHT and use them in the following ways:

1 Give a simple 'weather forecast', e.g. *Demain, il va faire chaud.*

A student places the correct symbol on the OHP.

---

2 Place all the symbols on the OHP. Lengthen the 'weather forecast', e.g.

Demain, il va faire du vent et il va pleuvoir.

A student covers on the OHP the symbols which are not described in your 'weather forecast', so that only the symbols you mentioned remain.

Further practice on this topic can be found in **Vital 1**, *Unité 4*.

USE OF ASSESSMENT WORKSHEETS

Worksheet 49

Dialogue 1
– Quel temps fait-il ici, en hiver?
– Il fait souvent du brouillard.

Dialogue 2
– Quel temps fait-il ici, en hiver?
– D'habitude il fait du soleil.

Dialogue 3
– Quel temps fait-il ici, en hiver?
– Il fait souvent du vent.

Dialogue 4
– Quel temps fait-il ici, en hiver?
– Il neige presque tous les jours.

Dialogue 5
– Quel temps fait-il ici, en hiver?
– Il fait souvent beau.

Dialogue 6
– Quel temps fait-il ici, en hiver?
– Il pleut souvent.

Dialogue 7
– Quel temps fait-il ici, en hiver?
– Il fait souvent très froid.

Worksheet 50

1
Dialogue 1
– Dis-moi, quel temps fait-il aujourd'hui chez toi, Mélanie?
– Il ne fait pas très beau. Il fait du vent.

Dialogue 2
– Dis-moi, quel temps fait-il aujourd'hui chez toi,Guillaume?
– Il fait très beau et il fait très chaud.

Dialogue 3
– Dis-moi, quel temps fait-il aujourd'hui chez toi, Céline?
– Il ne fait pas beau du tout. Il fait du brouillard.

Dialogue 4
– Dis-moi, quel temps fait-il aujourd'hui chez toi, Paul?
– Brr . . . il fait froid. Je ne vais pas en ville aujourd'hui.

Dialogue 5
– Dis-moi, quel temps fait-il aujourd'hui chez toi, Anne?
– Oh, il fait beau. Il fait du soleil.

2
a
– Quel temps fait-il en été, à Antibes?
– Il fait beau et il fait chaud.

b
– Quel temps fait-il en automne, en Normandie?
– Il pleut souvent et il fait du vent.

c
– Quel temps fait-il en hiver, à Chamonix?
– Il fait froid et il neige.

d
– Quel temps fait-il en hiver, à Carcassonne?
– Il fait beau et il fait du soleil.

Worksheets 51a and 51b

This is a pair-work activity where student A and student B have different worksheets. They must not look at each other's worksheet.

Worksheet 53

You may wish to discuss in English the sorts of answers students will need to write before they start this worksheet.

ANSWERS FOR ASSESSMENT WORKSHEETS

Worksheet 49
1 Boulogne; 2 Nice; 3 Bordeaux; 4 Grenoble; 5 Toulouse; 6 Lyons; 7 Calais.

Worksheet 50
1 a5; b4; c3; d1; e2.
2 a nice and hot; b rain and wind; c cold and snow; d nice and sun.

Worksheet 53
a nice and sunny; b cold, sun and snow; c because it's rainy and windy; d because it's foggy and cold.

Au travail

Objectives

- to talk about jobs.
- to talk about places of work.
- to give starting and finishing times.
- to understand information given in job adverts.

TEACHING NOTES

STUDENT'S BOOK, page 50

Introduce this unit by asking the students if they have any ideas about the kind of work they would like to have when they have left school. What kind of work did they, or will they do on their work experience programme?

Read through the jobs advertisements on this page and ask students to guess what any of the words mean, especially the words similar to the English, i.e. *mécanicien* or *électricien*. Give clues to the meaning of *vendeur* ('vending machines' or 'vendor' and 'buyer'), when moving house. What does *un job d'été* mean?

Give students clues by writing the names of the months of the summer on the board.

Background information

In the last century, most French people worked on the land. The great majority of the population in France was employed in farming or in crafts connected with agriculture. Today the situation has been reversed. Only a very small proportion (less than 5%) are occupied in farming. Many people are now working in man-ufacturing industries and the service industries.

STUDENT'S BOOK, page 51
Objective 1: to talk about jobs

Presenting the language

In order to keep this unit simple, we have selected seven jobs (*secrétaire, caissier, agent de police, professeur, facteur, infirmier, vendeur*). Students are only presented with both the masculine and feminine forms for *vendeur/vendeuse, caissier/caissière, infirmier/infirmière*. Show the students flashcards with symbols to denote the following jobs: *une secrétaire* (word processor and phone), *un agent de police* (handcuffs and baton) *un professeur* (OHP and OHP pens), *un caissier* (check-out till), *un facteur* (post-box and letter), *un infirmier* (person in white with red cross on hat), *un vendeur* (person in

local supermarket uniform). The students repeat the name of the job as the card is presented.

Show the flashcards again, this time asking *Qu'est-ce qu'il fait?*, to elicit the name of the job and supplying alternative answers if necessary.

Write the names of the jobs on cards. Stick the flashcards with the symbols onto the board. Time volunteers to see how long it takes to match the words with the symbols.

Activity 1

To familiarise students with the question, *Qu'est-ce qu' il fait dans la vie?*, use TV characters, e.g. PC Rowan ('Heartbeat'), Charlie Fairhead (nurse, 'Casualty'), Ken Barlow (teacher, 'Coronation Street').

Activity 2

Students are presented with three jobs. Before the students translate the captions into English, explain that *il* means 'he' and *elle* means 'she' (e.g. *il* for Neil; *elle* for Michelle) Ask the students, *June Ackland* (policewoman, The Bill) *qu'est-ce qu'elle fait dans la vie?*

Activity 3

a
– Ton père, qu'est-ce qu'il fait dans la vie?
– Il est agent de police.
– Ton père, qu'est-ce qu'il fait dans la vie?
– Il est professeur.
– Ton père, qu'est-ce qu'il fait dans la vie?
– Il est caissier.
– Ton père, qu'est-ce qu'il fait dans la vie?
– Il est facteur.

– Ta mère, qu'est-ce qu'elle fait dans la vie?
– Elle est secrétaire.
– Ta mère, qu'est-ce qu'elle fait dans la vie?
– Elle est vendeuse.

– Ta mère, qu'est-ce qu'elle fait dans la vie?
– Elle est infirmière.
– Ta mère, qu'est-ce qu'elle fait dans la vie?
– Elle est caissière.

Before students work on part **b** of the activity, remind them that they do not have to tell the truth to gain marks! The more persistent students can use dictionaries to find the words for more obscure professions or you can provide them with the vocabulary. The use of dictionaries is allowed in the GCSE examination and at any time for the Certificate of Achievement.

The answers to part **b** are: **A** *Il est infirmier*; **B** *Il est facteur*; **C** *Il est professeur*; **D** *Il/Elle est caissier/caissière*; **E** *Elle est secrétaire*.

Patterns of language

Explain that sometimes the names for the jobs change depending on whether the employee is male or female, as in English with actor and actress, steward and stewardess. Point out that the French do not say he or she is a nurse, they omit the *un* or *une* here.

STUDENT'S BOOK, page 52
Objective 2: to talk about places of work

Presenting the language

The vocabulary for this objective includes *dans un supermarché, dans un bureau, dans un hôpital* and *en ville*.

Revise the previous question *Ton père, qu'est-ce qu'il fait dans la vie?*, then extend this to include *Et il travaille où?* with, at this stage, alternative answers being the names of familiar towns. Practise this question in pairs.

Introduce the four places with flashcards. Repeat the question *Il travaille où?*, then show one of the flashcards, saying the name of the place in French. Practise the four places.

Divide an OHT into quarters. Each quarter has the name of one of the places of work written on it. Show the students the symbols used previously for the jobs. Cut the symbols and, using one at a time, ask the students where they think they should go; ask, for example,

Un vendeur – il travaille où? Place the symbol in the quarter marked *dans un supermarché.*

Activity 1
a
– Ta mère, qu'est-ce-qu'elle fait dans la vie?
– Elle travaille dans un hôpital.
– Ta mère, qu'est-ce qu'elle fait dans la vie?
– Elle travaille en ville.
– Ton père, qu'est-ce qu'il fait dans la vie?
– Il travaille dans un bureau.
– Ton père, qu'est-ce qu'il fait dans la vie?
– Il travaille dans un supermarché.

Do not attempt to do part **b** at the same time as the first part of the exercise.

b
– Mon père est facteur. Il travaille dans un hôpital. Faux!
– Ma mère est secrétaire. Elle travaille dans un bureau.
– Ma mère est infirmière. Elle travaille dans un super-marché.
– Mon père est caissier. Il travaille dans un bureau.
– Mon père est facteur. Il travaille en ville.

Activity 2

For further practice, the students make domino cards. On the left side of the card write the name of a job. On the right side write or draw a place of work. The cards can be matched word to word or word to picture as long as there is an agreed connection.

Activity 3

This can be set as a homework activity. Ask students to bring in at least one picture and to prepare in rough a caption to go with it. At the end of the next lesson, students can print out their captions on the computer.

STUDENT'S BOOK, pages 53–54
Objective 3: to give starting and finishing times

Presenting the language

Revise the numbers 1–24 (see strategies for teaching numbers on page 8). Explain that the words *heure* or *heures* are like hour and mean 'o'clock'.

Activity 1

If they need further practice with pronunciation, ask students for ideas for other 'voices' (e.g. talking clock, etc.). Let individuals repeat individual sentences in a different voice and the rest of the class has to decide who it is.

a
– A une heure, le train pour. . .
– A sept heures, le train pour. . .
– A huit heures, le train pour. . .
– A neuf heures, le train pour. . .
– A treize heures, le train pour. . .
– A quinze heures, le train pour. . .
– A seize heures, le train pour. . .
– A dix-sept heures, le train pour. . .
– A dix-huit heures, le train pour. . .

b

1	**4**
– Alors, à 2 heures.	– Alors, à 9 heures.
– Oui, à 2 heures!	– Oui, à 9 heures!
2	**5**
– Alors, à 7 heures.	– Alors, à 9 heures 30.
– Oui, à 7 heures!	– Oui, à 9 heures 30!
3	
– Alors, à 10 heures.	
– Oui, à 10 heures!	

c

1 Il est 7 heures.	**6** Il est 14 heures.
2 Il est 6 heures.	**7** Il est 19 heures.
3 Il est 11 heures 30.	**8** Il est 13 heures.
4 Il est 5 heures.	**9** Il est 20 heures 30.
5 Il est 3 heures 30.	

Activity 2

Look at the TV programme extract with the students and work through the programmes that are on TV that day.

Draw the students' attention to the similarity to the English. What does 'commence' mean in English?

Differentiation   More able students can make up further questions for their partner or do a written translation of the day's programmes.

Activity 3

Note that some students may need the 24-hour clock to be explained.

Activity 4

Ask students to invent their own dialogue using personal details or making up an imaginary scenario. Some students may have difficulty working the whole dialogue. If this is the case, break it down for them so that they practise the first four sentences thoroughly before moving onto the last four. They may actually prefer to write out their new dialogue before attempting to role-play it. You may need to help them identify the words to be substituted. More able students could perfect their role-play and perform it.

Activity 5

Work the first question with your students to ensure comprehension.

b
– La secrétaire commence à 9 heures.
– Le professeur commence à 8 heures.
– La secrétaire finit à 17 heures.
– Le professeur finit à 16 heures.

Differentiation   More able students could write out more examples of these questions.

Point out to the students that, as in the GCSE examination, it is not necessary to understand every single word and that they should learn to pick out the words they already know or that they can guess.

Activity 1

Go over the questions in French orally so that those students needing support can listen to alternative answers in the first place. Photocopy this page onto an OHT and ask the students to come to the front, one at a time, and underline (in non-permanent ink) any word or phrase that they can recognise and translate for the rest of the class.

Differentiation   The less able write the letter of the correct answer. The more able write a complete sentence. The more able could go on to produce a sketch which involves all the components of the summary page. This could be along the lines of a girlfriend or boyfriend meeting their partners' parents for the first time. The parents are inquisitive, wanting to know where each parent works, etc. Alternatively, the students could pretend to meet a penfriend and they want to discover what the penfriend's parents do for a living.

Explain the context in English but emphasise that all the dialogue has to be in French.

TRANSITION TO GCSE

This unit only introduces a small number of jobs. Check your GCSE syllabus for the defined list. Students will only need to say or write jobs which apply to their family and friends. All other jobs can be taught for recognition only. If students' friends and family have jobs which are difficult to remember, they can avoid the problem by using *Il/Elle travaille chez. . . .*

Many of the jobs on the defined list for GCSE are cognates or near-cognates. Draw students' attention to this and to the fact that they should look out for such words in their reading exam at GCSE. Often they will be able to link words in this way to English and make a guess

as to the meaning, e.g. *dentiste; garagiste; médecin; chauffeur.*

Students will gain extra marks if they can state jobs they have done and state an opinion of that job. Both these can be achieved extremely simply.

J'ai travaillé dans un magasin.
C'était intéressant, nul, etc.

In addition, students should learn to say what they want to do when they leave school.

Je voudrais travailler dans un bureau.

Further practice on this topic can be found in **Vital 2**, *Unité 2* and *Unité 3*.

USE OF ASSESSMENT WORKSHEETS

Worksheet 56
1
Dialogue 1
– Qu'est-ce que vous faites dans la vie?
– Moi, je travaille comme facteur. Je travaille en ville.
Dialogue 2
– Qu'est-ce que vous faites dans la vie?
– Je suis vendeur dans un grand magasin à Paris.

Dialogue 3
– Qu'est-ce que vous faites dans la vie?
– Je travaille dans un bureau. Je suis secrétaire.
Dialogue 4
– Qu'est-ce que vous faites dans la vie?
– Je suis caissière dans un hypermarché.
Dialogue 5
– Qu'est-ce que vous faites dans la vie?
– Je suis infirmière dans un hôpital à Nice.

Dialogue 6
– Qu'est-ce que vous faites dans la vie?
– Je suis agent de police. Je travaille dans le centre-ville.

2
Moi, je travaille dans un collège. Je suis professeur.

Worksheet 57

Dialogue 1
– Vous commencez votre travail à quelle heure?
– Je commence mon travail à 8 heures.

Dialogue 2
– Vous commencez votre travail à quelle heure?
– Ça dépend. D'habitude, je commence mon travail à 14 heures.

Dialogue 3
– Vous commencez votre travail à quelle heure?
– D'habitude, je commence mon travail à 8 heures et demie.

Dialogue 4
– Vous commencez votre travail à quelle heure?
– D'habitude, je commence mon travail à 9 heures.

Dialogue 5
– Vous commencez votre travail à quelle heure?
– D'habitude, je commence mon travail à 7 heures et demie.

Dialogue 6
– Vous commencez votre travail à quelle heure?
– D'habitude, je commence mon travail à 20 heures.

Dialogue 7
– Vous commencez votre travail à quelle heure?
– D'habitude, je commence mon travail à minuit.

Dialogue 8
– Vous commencez votre travail à quelle heure?
– D'habitude, je commence mon travail à 11 heures et demie.

Worksheet 58

1
Dialogue 1
– Marie, qu'est-ce que vous faites dans la vie?
– Je suis infirmière. Je travaille dans un hôpital.
– Oh, c'est intéressant.

Dialogue 2
– Jean-Paul, qu'est-ce que vous faites dans la vie?
– Moi, je suis vendeur dans un magasin. Je travaille en ville.
– Vous aimez ça?
– Oui, c'est bien.

Dialogue 3
– Roger, qu'est-ce que vous faites dans la vie?
– Je suis secrétaire. Je travaille dans un bureau.
– Tiens! Moi aussi.

Dialogue 4
– Anne, est-ce que tu travailles dans le centre-ville?
– Non, je travaille dans la banlieue. Je travaille dans un grand supermarché. Je suis caissière.
– Caissière. . . ma sœur est caissière, elle aussi.

2
– Ton amie, Nicole, qu'est-ce qu'elle fait dans la vie?
– Elle travaille en ville. Elle est vendeuse dans un grand magasin.
– Elle commence son travail à quelle heure?
– A 9 heures.
– Et elle finit à quelle heure?
– Vers 18 heures. Et ton ami, David, il travaille aussi dans le centre-ville?
– Non, David travaille dans un hôpital près du centre-ville.
– Il commence son travail de très bonne heure?
– Ça dépend. D'habitude, il commence son travail à 14 heures et il finit à 22 heures.
– Ah, ça va.

ANSWERS FOR ASSESSMENT WORKSHEETS

Worksheet 56
1 a3; b4; c6; d1; e5; f2.
2 = teacher.

Worksheet 57
1 8.00; 2 14.00; 3 8.30; 4 9.00; 5 7.30; 6 20.00;
7 midnight; 8 11.30.

Worksheet 58
1 1b; 2c; 3c; 4c.
2 1 shop; 2 sales person; 3 9 a.m.; 4 6 p.m.; 5 2 p.m.;
  6 hospital.

Worksheet 61
a In town; b Postman; c midday; d hospital; e nurse;
f midnight; g office; h 9.30.

Worksheet 62
1 b, 2 c; 3 a; 4 d; 5 10 p.m.; 6 1.30 p.m.; 7 9 o' clock;
8 5.30 p.m.

Les vêtements

Objectives

- to ask for an item of clothing.
- to buy an item of clothing.

TEACHING NOTES

STUDENT'S BOOK, page 57

Read the objectives to your students. Ask if they recognise the designer names from the picture and if they can name any more. Discuss the importance of clothes in their lives. How much money do they spend on them?, etc. Ask if they can think why High Street fashion should be similar across Europe (satellite TV, film, travel, etc).

Ask students what they know about French currency. If possible, bring in a selection of coins and notes and discuss their approximate worth in English money. Highlight the importance of being able to understand and roughly convert French currency, when shopping in France.

Background information

High Street fashion is much the same now in France as in the UK and the rest of Europe. Shops that are popular in France as well as in the UK include Benetton and Marks & Spencer. French people are generally interested in clothes and tend to like good quality clothing – even teenagers will forego a large wardrobe for quality.

STUDENT'S BOOK, pages 58–59
Objective 1: to ask for an item of clothing

Presenting the language

Bring in a bag of clothing in differing colours and sizes. Make the presentation humourous by using a mixture of fashionable, old-fashioned, baby and outsize clothes. Introduce the cognates first, moving on to the less obvious vocabulary when students are ready.

Consolidate the new language through the use of interactive games, e.g.

- 'Mock auction': one student selects and holds up an item of clothing. The first student to name it, gets it (to ensure the participation of all students, limit the game to one item each).

- 'Quick on the draw': a volunteer begins to draw an item of clothing on the OHP. The first student to name it, takes the next turn (again, one student, one turn).

Activity 1

Make sure that all students are well prepared for the listening exercise by firstly looking at the illustrations and ask them to point to the item of clothing that each person is wearing as you name it. Students then listen to the tape and decide which person is being described.

NB Although students will not be assessed on *je porte. . .* , it may be useful to introduce it to them at this stage as it will allow you to present the words which will be assessed in a more realistic context.

a
1 Moi, je porte un pantalon.
2 Moi, je porte une veste.
3 Moi, je porte un jogging.

When they have completed the listening exercise and you have checked it over with them, move on to the repetition exercise. If they need more practice with this, replay the tape and ask them to repeat the whole sentence slowly each time.

b
– Moi, je porte un pantalon.
– Moi, je porte un jogging.
– Moi, je porte une veste.

Differentiation Less able students may need more listening and repetition practice before they feel comfortable with the new vocabulary. If so, let them listen to the tape again through the headphones. Meanwhile, for the more able, draw a grid on the OHP, showing the three items of clothing from the exercise: *pantalon/veste/jogging*. Students copy the grid and fill in the name of the person wearing that item.

Activity 2

You will need to brainstorm this in English with the students so as to elicit ideas for clothing they deem suitable for each age group.

When you feel that students are confident with the vocabulary, you could extend this work by asking them to write a description of what one or more of the models on the page is wearing. Alternatively, they could bring in a picture of their favourite famous personality (it usually helps to have a supply from latest teenage/pop/ sports magazines) and describe what he or she is wearing.

Activity 3

Practise *je voudrais* with students by giving out items of clothing and asking for them back.

Elicit meaning from the students and then give them the opportunity to practise by asking you for their favourite item from the bag.

Discuss the idea of different clothing for different occasions. Hold up an item and ask the students *C'est O.K. pour le cinéma/le match de football?*, etc. Exploit this with humour, holding up inappropriate items, too!

Differentiation Less able students may only have time to write out the answer of their choice. For more able students who finish the exercise quickly, have a back up activity: prepare an OHT showing a grid with clothing down the left column and various places (use cognates: *le match, le cinéma, le restaurant, le supermarché*, etc.) along the top of the other columns. Students can copy this grid into their books and tick the places that they consider each item of clothing suitable for.

Activity 4

Work through the language of the promotion with the students to elicit meaning. Explain that they do not have to understand every word and that it is an achievement if they can just understand the gist. Ask students to work in pairs to 'telephone' their order.

Patterns of language

Point out that, as with all nouns in French, some words for clothing are masculine and some are feminine. This has nothing to do with clothing being suitable for men or women!

STUDENT'S BOOK, pages 60–61
Objective 2: to buy an item of clothing

Presenting the language

Introduce the colours first, using classroom items – felt tip pens, crayons, etc. are ideal for this. Present the cognates first, moving on to the less obvious and ask students to think of ways to memorise the vocabulary (*jaune* = yellow, jaundice, etc.). Encourage them to use colours in everyday classroom language.

Move on to introduce *taille*. Again use the bag of clothing (see suggestions for use on page 46) to demonstrate *grand, petit* and *moyen*.

Now introduce *C'est combien?* and give the students plenty of practice with this.

Revise the numbers, especially the tens and hundreds. Put price tags on the clothing so that the practice is more meaningful, or ask each student what they think each item should cost (encourage realistic prices).

Activity 1

When you are happy that the students are familiar with the colours and sizes and know

---

how to ask the price of something, present them with the flow chart.

Activity 2

Differentiation Students may need you to break the dialogue down for them into more manageable chunks. Let them practise each set of questions and answers several times before moving on to the next. Ask them to start at the beginning each time they are to add a new chunk, so as to avoid confusion and so that they see their own progression more clearly.

Activity 3

Students now make conversations based on the model dialogue. Challenge them to either write more than five sentences or to write five in a set time!

The students have learned a lot of new language so far in this unit and it may be worthwhile to give them an opportunity to consolidate this before moving on. Do this through games, such as 'Le shopping': make sets of cards, each card containing a picture of one item of clothing. (Students could make their own cards, using mail-order catalogues.) Students work in pairs, each with an identical set of cards. A asks for an item from his/her pile. B finds the item from his/her pile. This game can be made more difficult for more able students by grouping them into 'departments' selling different items in different sizes, colours, etc. Students have a list and they have to move around from department to department. The shopkeepers then have to ask *Quelle taille?*, etc.

Activity 4

Before beginning activity 4, brainstorm students for the vocabulary of the unit in categories: colours, sizes, etc.

Add humour to the repetition activities by asking for volunteers to repeat one of the decriptions again in a different voice, e.g. high-class fashion salesperson, marketstall holder.

a & b
– Un pantalon. Taille: grand, petit. Couleurs: noir, bleu, vert.
– Un sweat. Taille: grand, petit. Couleurs: jaune, rouge.
– Un jogging. Taille: moyen, petit. Couleurs: noir, bleu.
– Un tee-shirt. Taille: moyen, petit. Couleurs: rouge, bleu, noir.

Before moving on to activity 4c, revise the numbers again thoroughly. Use the bag of clothing again to offer plenty of practice with prices.

Play 'The price is right'. One student selects an item of clothing from the bag and describes it, making sure not to let the class see its price tag. A second student suggests a price for the item. The rest of the class calls out *Oui!* or *Non!* according to what they think the item is worth. You then check the price of the item to see who was right.

c
– Un tee-shirt, c'est combien?
– 100 francs.
– 100 francs?
– Oui, 100 francs.

– Un jean, c'est combien?
– 200 francs.
– 200 francs?
– Oui, 200 francs.

– Un sweat, c'est combien?
– 150 francs.
– 150 francs?
– Oui, 150 francs.

– Une casquette, c'est combien?
– 40 francs.
– 40 francs?
– Oui, 40 francs.

– Un pull, c'est combien?
– 120 francs.
– 120 francs?
– 120 francs.

Differentiation Students could find pictures of the items mentioned in activity 4c from mail-order catalogues, cut them out and label them with prices. More able students could extend the activity by deciding whether the prices given for each item were reasonable (they will need help with conversion). They could then make two lists in their books (*cher/pas cher*) and place the items in the appropriate lists. Remember, however, that they will not be assessed on this extra language.

Activity 5

Less able students will need help 'spending' their 300 francs. (If you have access to calculators, this will help.)

Activity 6

Less able students may need extra support with this. Give them a framework from which to work by brainstorming and then writing on the OHP what the first exchange would be.

Activity 7

It is useful if you have a supply of catalogues for students to use for their own catalogue.

Differentiation will be by outcome. The more able the student, the more detailed and numerous their catalogue descriptions will be.

It is often very enjoyable and motivating for students to round off this unit of work with a fashion show. Students work in pairs to write the script for their presentation, e.g.*Voici Kelly, elle porte. . . .* Students are not assessed on their use of the phrase *il/elle porte. . . .*

TRANSITION TO GCSE

This unit covers the majority of the phrases needed for GCSE. In addition, students will need to be able to:

- express simple opinions about clothes. *J'aime ce jean.*

- say they will/will not buy something. *Je prends ce pull.* *C'est trop cher (petit) (grand).*

Check your GCSE syllabus for the full list of clothes and colours. Students will need to know all these for the role-plays.

Students will also need to understand signs to be found in shops and department stores. Check your GCSE syllabus for the defined list.

Further practice on this topic can be found in **Vital 2**, *Unité 8*.

USE OF ASSESSMENT WORKSHEETS

Worksheet 63

If students have problems drawing Robert's clothing, they can show their comprehension through English answers.

Dialogue 1
– Voici une photo de moi. Regarde! Je porte mon nouveau pantalon et ma nouvelle veste.

Dialogue 2
– C'est moi. Comme toujours je porte une jupe, et un pull.

Dialogue 3
– J'aime porter une casquette, un jean et un tee-shirt.

2
– Je m'appelle Robert. J'aime porter un jean, un pull et une veste. . . et je porte toujours une casquette.

Worksheet 64

1
– Bonjour. Vous désirez?
– Je voudrais un jean.
– De quelle couleur?
– Bleu.

– Et quelle taille?
– Petit.
– Voilà. C'est tout?
– Non. Je voudrais aussi une veste.
– De quelle couleur?
– Noire.
– Et quelle taille?
– Moyen.
– Voilà. C'est tout?
– Non. Je voudrais aussi une casquette.
– De quelle couleur?
– Bleue.
– Et quelle taille?
– Grand.
– Voilà. C'est tout?
– Non. Je voudrais aussi un tee-shirt.
– De quelle couleur?
– Blanc.
– Et quelle taille?
– Petit.
– Voilà. C'est tout?
– Oui, c'est tout! Ça fait combien?
– Ça fait 900 francs!
– 900 francs! Oh, là là!

2
– Je vais en ville.
– Qu'est-ce que tu veux acheter?
– Je vais acheter une jupe.
– Oh, de quelle couleur?
– Je vais acheter une jupe noire pour ma sœur.
– Et tu vas aussi acheter des vêtements pour toi?
– Oui, je voudrais acheter une casquette.
– De quelle couleur?
– Je voudrais acheter une casquette noire.
– Oh, c'est bien. C'est tout?
– Non, je voudrais aussi acheter un tee-shirt pour mon ami. Je voudrais acheter un grand tee-shirt blanc.
– Oh, tu as beaucoup de choses à acheter. Je te souhaite bonne chance!
– Merci.

Worksheet 65

Dialogue 1
– Bonjour. Vous désirez?
– Ce tee-shirt. C'est combien, s'il vous plaît?
– C'est 105 francs, monsieur.
– 105 francs. . . merci, et ce pull. C'est combien?
– C'est 210 francs, monsieur.
– Mm. . . 210 francs. . . et cette casquette. C'est combien?
– C'est 100 francs, monsieur.

– 100 francs. . . alors, je prends cette casquette et le tee-shirt, s'il vous plaît.
– Très bien, monsieur.

Dialogue 2
– Bonjour. Cette jupe, c'est combien, s'il vous plaît?
– C'est 200 francs, mademoiselle.
– 200 francs. . . et ce pantalon c'est combien?
– C'est 120 francs, mademoiselle.
– Mm. . . 120 francs. . . et cette veste c'est combien?
– C'est 300 francs, mademoiselle.
– Alors, la jupe, s'il vous plaît.

Worksheet 66

Practise the dialogue in class before students work in pairs.

Worksheet 68

Students will need colours to complete this task. It will be helpful if you have a supply of the following colours: black, blue, red, green, yellow, brown.

Worksheet 69

It is not necessary for students to have correct adjectival agreement to achieve the outcome.

ANSWERS FOR ASSESSMENT WORKSHEETS

Worksheet 63
1 1 Anne; 2 Nicole; 3 Sophie.
2 Robert = jeans, pullover, jacket, cap.

Worksheet 64
1 small blue jeans, black medium-sized jacket, large blue cap, small white t-shirt.
2 Une jupe noire, une casquette noire, un grand tee-shirt blanc.

Worksheet 65
t-shirt 105F, pullover 210F, cap 100F, skirt 200F, trousers 120F, jacket 300F.

Worksheet 67
1 1 C, 2 A, 3 D, 4 B.
2 a medium and small; b white, green, yellow, red, black; c large and small; d red, blue, green; e blue, black, white; f 200F.

Worksheet 68
b blue pullover; c large red sweatshirt; d green skirt; e small white tracksuit; f black trousers; g large yellow cap; h large brown trousers.

Chez moi

Objectives

- to describe your home.
- to talk about the rooms in your home.
- to write about homes.

TEACHING NOTES

STUDENT'S BOOK, page 63

Read the objectives to your students. Ask if they can pick out any familiar words or guess what any of the words in the adverts mean. Some of the French words describing housing are used in the English language such as maisonette, chalet, and apartment. What do these words mean? What is a *gîte* or a *château*?

Background information

Many people in France live in flats. On the edge of big towns there are huge blocks of modern flats called HLM, which means *habitations à loyers modérés* (homes with a moderate rent). These were built to try and ease a widespread shortage of housing. Whole new towns have also been created. A higher proportion of French than British people rent their house.

STUDENT'S BOOK, pages 64–65
Objective 1: to describe your home

Presenting the language

For this objective, the students will need to actively know *un appartement, une maison, grand(e)* and *petit(e)*.

Before moving to the first activity, show the students general pictures of things that are large or small, such as an elephant and a mouse. The students say either *grand* or *petit* and place the pictures into two corresponding piles.

Ask the students *Tu habites dans un maison ou dans un appartement?* Elicit the active response *J'habite dans....* Ask whether the house is small or large, offering them the alternatives and nothing else at this stage.

Activity 1

Explain to the students that correct pronunciation leads to a linking of *petit* and *appartement* because *appartement* begins with a vowel.

a & b

– J'habite dans un petit appartement à Paris.
– J'habite dans une petite maison à Cannes.
– J'habite dans une grande maison.
– J'habite dans un grand appartement à Nice.

Differentiation   Practise the language more with those who need it by showing them various house pictures from an estate agent's. The student can repeat *La maison est grande* before you move onto asking them at random whether the houses and flats are big or small.

Patterns of language

Il and *elle* can mean 'he' and 'she'. They can also mean 'it'. A word following *le* or *un* will be *il*, and following *la* or *une* it will be *elle*, e.g. *un appartement – il est grand*.

Activity 2

Practise this dialogue one line at a time with the students first. They can then work the dialogue in pairs. If some students find the dialogue too long, allow them to break it down so that they use the first two lines only at first. They can then build this up, starting from the beginning each time.

Students can write the words in an original way to help memorise them visually, such as *maison* or *appartement*. The most original can go on display.

Differentiation   For the more able, set an oral or written quiz in French, e.g. Où habite Paula Yates, Liam Gallagher, Bill Clinton et Salman Rushdie?

STUDENT'S BOOK, page 66
Objective 2: to talk about the rooms in your home

The vocabulary for this objective is *le salon, la salle à manger, la chambre, la salle de bains* and *la cuisine*.

Presenting the language

If you have the time and resources, video a showhouse or your own house with very basic commentary in French, e.g. *Il y a une cuisine. Elle est grande*, etc. A French visitor or a young child doing the commentary in French adds to the interest. The students watch the video a second time without the sound and repeat the words after the teacher.

Activity 1

Look at the photographs. Ask the students to repeat the words after you.

1 Il y a une salle à manger.
2 Il y a une salle de bains.
3 Il y a un salon.
4 Il y a une cuisine.
5 Il y a une chambre.

Activity 2
a

1 Il y a. . . deux salons, une cuisine, une salle à manger, quatre chambres et deux salles de bains.
2 Il y a. . . un salon, une cuisine, une chambre, une salle de bains et une salle à manger.
3 Il y a. . . un salon, une cuisine, un coin feu, une salle à manger, une salle de bains et deux chambres.

Differentiation   More able students who finish early could listen to the tape again through headphones and take notes on the other descriptions.

Activity 3

Elicit the active use of *grande* or *petite* from the more able students. Students can draw items of furniture, or if you wish, use familiar sounding words for items of furniture orally. At this stage students' answers need only be the names of rooms, e.g. *C'est pour quelle pièce? La salle de bains ou le salon?* Students are not assessed on using vocabulary for items of furniture, but if you wish to, you could extend their work in this direction.

STUDENT'S BOOK, page 67
Objective 3: to write about homes

Revise the words for rooms orally. Revise the numbers 1–5 orally. Ask the question *Il y a combien de chambres dans ta maison?*, emphasising to the students that the truth is not absolutely necessary!

Activity 1

Before the students describe the house, the teacher gives a role model, e.g. *Oui, il y a 4 chambres. Il y a une salle de bains et une grande salle à manger. La cuisine est grande, oui.*

Activity 2

After translating the advert into English, the more able could be encouraged to translate an authentic advert from a local estate agent's into French. Emphasise that they should concentrate on key words only.

Le sommaire
Ideas for revision Use the computer software (available in most schools in the special needs department) 'My World' or 'Le monde à moi' to label the rooms in the house and print out.

Copy a plan of a house but label it in mirror writing and ask the students to decipher it.

Play 'Through the key-hole' with a photo of one room in a house from helpful members of staff. Which teacher's *salon* or *salle de bains* is this?

TRANSITION TO GCSE

To achieve the objectives for GCSE, students will need to be able to:

- state whether they have a garden.
  J'ai un (grand/petit) jardin.
  Je n'ai pas de jardin.

- state whether they have a garage.
  J'ai une garage pour une (deux) voiture(s).
  Je n'ai pas de garage.

- give details of rooms.
  Ma chambre est petite.
  Ma chambre est bleue.
  Il y a un lit, une table et une télé.

Check your GCSE syllabus for the items of furniture on the defined syllabus.

To practise the words for room contents, play 'le jeu des blancs'. Students work in two teams. One student from team A comes to the front. Give all students in team A an incomplete sentence, for example, *Dans le salon, il y a . . .* They decide how to complete the sentence and write it in full. The student at the front writes his/her complete sentence on the board. The other students from team A then read out their sentences. Team A scores a point from each sentence read out which matches the sentence on the board. Repeat the activity with team B.

Further practice on this topic can be found in **Vital 1**, *Unité 9*.

USE OF ASSESSMENT WORKSHEETS

Worksheet 71
Dialogue 1
– Tu habites dans une maison ou dans un appartement?
– J'habite dans une maison au bord de la mer.
– Ta maison, elle est grande?
– Non, elle est petite.
– Tu peux décrire la maison?
– Oui. Il y a un salon, une cuisine, deux salles de bains et deux chambres.
Dialogue 2
– Tu habites dans une maison ou dans un appartement?
– J'habite dans un appartement dans le centre-ville.
– Ton appartement, il est grand?

– Non, il est petit.
– Tu peux décrire l'appartement?
– Oui. Il y a un petit salon, une toute petite cuisine, une salle de bains et une chambre.
– C'est pratique, hein?
– Oui, c'est très pratique.
Dialogue 3
– Où habites-tu maintenant?
– Nous avons acheté une maison à la campagne.
– Ah, bon. . . une maison. Elle est grande ou petite?
– Euh. . . elle est assez grande.
– Elle est comment, ta nouvelle maison?
– Alors, elle est assez grande. Il y a le salon, la salle à manger, la cuisine, la salle de bains et trois chambres.
– Ah, c'est bien.

Dialogue 4

– Tu habites dans une maison ou dans un appartement?
– J'habite une maison.
– Elle est grande ou petite?
– Elle est grande.
– Il y a combien de pièces?
– Il y a un grand salon avec vue sur la piscine, il y a la salle à manger. . . il y a naturellement une cuisine. . . il y a quatre chambres. . .et deux salles de bains.
– Tu aimes la maison?
– Oui, je l'aime bien.

Worksheet 72

1

Dialogue 1

– Nous avons ici un appartement dans le centre-ville. C'est très pratique.
– Vous avez une photo?
– Oui, un instant, s'il vous plaît.

Dialogue 2

– Regardez. C'est vraiment une grande maison.
– Oh, oui, elle est très jolie.

Dialogue 3

– Voici le plan de l'appartement. Il y a deux chambres, le salon, la cuisine et une salle de bains.
– Ah, ça, c'est intéressant.

Dialogue 4

– Nous avons une maison près d'un village. Elle est assez grande. Il y a quatre chambres, un salon, la salle à manger, une cuisine et une salle de bains.
– Ah! Intéressant. Vous avez une photo de la maison?
– Un instant, madame. Je vais voir.

2

– Voici une photo de ma nouvelle maison.
– Oh, elle est grande!
– Oui, elle est assez grande.
– Il y a combien de pièces?
– Bon, il y a la cuisine...une grande cuisine...un salon . . . trois chambres. . . et deux salles de bains.
– Trois chambres et deux salles de bains. C'est bien, ça.

Worksheet 75

In each advert there are words which students do not need to understand.

Worksheet 78

Activity 2 is not an assessed activity.

ANSWERS FOR ASSESSMENT WORKSHEETS

Worksheet 71

2 appartement, petit, salon, cuisine, 1 salle de bains, 1 chambre.
3 maison, grande, salon, salle à manger, cuisine, 1 salle de bains, 3 chambres.
4 maison, grande, salon, salle à manger, cuisine, 4 chambres, 2 salles de bains.

Worksheet 72

1 a2; b1; c3; d4.
2 kitchen, lounge, 3 bedrooms, 2 bathrooms.

Worksheet 75

a 3; b 1; c 4; d2; e 2; f 1.

Worksheet 76

1 house; large; house; dining-room, kitchen, 2 bathrooms, 3 bedrooms.
2 flat; small; flat; lounge, kitchen, bathroom, one bedroom.
3 house, lounge, dining-room, kitchen, 4 bedrooms.

On fait les courses

Objectives
- to shop for food.
- to ask for prices.

TEACHING NOTES

STUDENT'S BOOK, page 69

Introduce this unit by asking students what kinds of groceries they would buy if they were camping in France.

Look at the photographs and decide what can be bought in each shop. *Boulangeries* sell *baguettes*; *patisseries* sell pastries and cakes.

Although it could be argued that it is possible to go into a large supermarket and serve oneself, stress to students the satisfaction they would feel if they could ask for and buy things in shops, using their knowledge of French.

Find out if any of the students have been to France. If so, where did they shop for groceries? Why is it that so many English people cross the Channel to go shopping?

Ask the students if they know how many French francs £1 would buy. Stress the importance of understanding French currency and being able to convert prices in France.

Background information

In France, huge *hypermarchés* have been built outside towns, as in Britain with 'out of town' shopping centres. The bargains are so good that even people from England drive over to France to shop there. Many French people prefer the old shops and are now concerned that hyper-markets may put some small shops out of business. Well known hypermarkets include Mammouth and Géant.

Nearly every French town has a market (*le marché*). The largest towns have markets every day and the smaller towns once a week.

There are still many small shops which are family-owned and run. These shops stay open late in order to compete. *Boulangeries* open very early in the morning because French people like to have fresh bread for breakfast (this even applies on Sundays). They bake again in the afternoon so that the bread is fresh for dinner! The price of bread in France is laid down by the government.

STUDENT'S BOOK, pages 70–71
Objective 1: to shop for food

Presenting the language

Explain in French *Je vais au supermarché; je voudrais un kilo de bananes.* Divide an OHT into quarters. In one of the quarters write *un kilo de. . . .* Say the other items to be bought:

Je voudrais. . . un paquet de/deux tranches de/une bouteille de. . . .

Write these into the remaining four squares. When the four squares are labelled, ask the students what they can buy. Some may need prompting, e.g. *Je voudrais une bouteille de bananes ou de coca?* Explain *200 grammes*. If they need to revise numbers, look at Unit 1 for ideas.

Bring in visual aids such as empty packets, plastic bottles and plastic fruit and food. Put four different bags or baskets on the table, labelled with categories. Time two volunteers how long it takes to sort the food and bottles into the correct categories. One volunteer says the item, the other places it in the bag.

Copy the flow chart in different coloured pens according to the category.

Activity 1

For further practice, play the tape again, pausing after each item and asking the students to say which category it belongs in.

a & b

– Je voudrais. . .
  un kilo de bananes
  un paquet de chips
  une bouteille de coca-cola
  2 tranches de jambon
  un kilo de poires
  une bouteille d'orangina
  un kilo de pommes
  200g de fromage
  une bouteille d'eau minérale
  un kilo de pêches
  un paquet de biscuits
  un kilo de tomates

Activity 2

Remind the students what the words *mange* and *boit* mean by miming and giving examples. Say some of the items and the students say *mange* or *boit*, e.g. *un coca on boit*.

2

– Je voudrais. . .
  un kilo de bananes
  un paquet de chips
  une bouteille de coca-cola
  2 tranches de jambon
  un kilo de poires
  une bouteille d'orangina
  un kilo de pommes
  200g de fromage
  une bouteille d'eau minérale
  un kilo de pêches
  un paquet de biscuits
  un kilo de tomates

Differentiation   Extend this activity for more able students by asking them to write a further list (they could write out what they think their partner's list could be and compare it afterwards) or by challenging them to write five or more words from memory.

STUDENT'S BOOK, page 72

Activity 3

a

1
– Bonjour, madame. Vous désirez?
– Je voudrais une baguette, s'il vous plaît.
– Et avec ça?
– Deux tranches de jambon.
– C'est tout?
– Oui.

2
– Bonjour, madame. Vous désirez?
– Je voudrais un kilo de tomates et un kilo de pêches, s'il vous plaît.
– Et avec ça?
– 200g de fromage.
– C'est tout?
– Oui.

3
– Bonjour, madame. Vous désirez?
– Je voudrais une bouteille de coca et un paquet de chips, s'il vous plaît.
– Et avec ça?
– Une bouteille d'orangina.
– C'est tout?
– Oui.

Differentiation   Some less able students may need support. Instead of their writing a list, have the items on cards and ask the students to select the correct cards and put them into the three lists. Practise by role-playing beforehand so that these students can visualise exactly what the task involves. If time allows, ask them to write out one list.

More able students who finish early could play the 'Au marché, j'ai acheté. . .' game by trying to memorise the items in each list with a partner.

For part **b** of the activity, ask the students to add a little drama. They could pretend to be a young child asking for sweets and more sweets or an elderly lady asking for a tiny bit of everything (e.g. *une banane, une tranche de fromage, deux tomates*, etc.).

In part **c** of the activity, you may need to brainstorm the students for foods appropriate to each situation.

Activity 4

For further practice, make up a *chariot C*. Students say what goes in the trolley. They then have ten seconds to memorise before writing down as many of the items as they can remember.

Differentiation   For those pupils who have difficulty writing, sketches, symbols or using the word cards will serve as alternatives.

Patterns of language

Point out that the expression *Je voudrais* is used again when asking for items in shops – it is so useful that it should be learned by heart!

Point out, too, that most of the quantities are followed by *de* (*un kilo de. . . , une tranche de. . . , une bouteille de. . . , 200g de. . .*). This becomes *d'* before a vowel (e.g. *bouteille d'orangina*).

STUDENT'S BOOK, page 73
Objective 2: to ask for prices

Activity 1
a
– Une bouteille de coca, c'est combien?
– Une bouteille de coca, ça fait 14 francs.
– 14 francs?
– Oui, 14 francs.

– 3 bananes, c'est combien?
– 3 bananes, ça fait 6 francs.
– 6 francs?
– Oui, 6 francs.

– Un paquet de biscuits, c'est combien?
– Un paquet de biscuits, ça fait 4 francs.
– 4 francs?
– Oui, 4 francs.

– 200g de fromage, c'est combien?
– 200g de fromage, ça fait 20 francs.
– 20 francs?
– Oui, 20 francs.

For activity 1b, students can use calculators if they feel discouraged because of the maths.

Activity 2

Go through the activity orally at first.

Differentiation   For the less able students, be ready with some questions in English, e.g.

1 How much is a packet of crisps?
2 How much is orange juice?

3 How much is 4 slices of ham?
4 What did the All-Bran cost?
5 What was bought for 6 francs?

For further practice, make posters such as can be found in supermarkets, to advertise the items of food with prices. Use authentic leaflets from local supermarkets which can be cut up and translated.

Activity 3

Students role-play their dialogues. Ask them to imagine realistic contexts, such as shopping for an elderly relative.

For further practice play 'Chinese whispers' in French. Ask for more than one item so that it taxes the memory as well as hearing and speaking skills.

If possible, show slides of food bought in France. See if individual students can say what they all are.

Play 'Quick on the draw': students volunteer to copy an item on a card given by the teacher onto the OHP for their team to guess. The team has five seconds to guess.

STUDENT'S BOOK, page 74

Le sommaire

To consolidate the language of the unit, stage a mock 'market auction' in French. Display the plastic fruit, vegetables, cheese and ham as well as empty plastic bottles and packets. Photocopy French banknotes and use real coins. Give each student the same amount (about 100 francs). One student holds up an item at the front and asks *C'est combien, une bouteille de coca-cola?* Students put in their bids in French until the 'auctioneer' says the price with *Un, deux, trois – une bouteille de coca-cola, 20F pour Madame X.*

In unit 1, students are taught the numbers 1–20. In this unit, they are taught to say 200g.

See which student can buy the most items for 100 francs!

TRANSITION TO GCSE

You will need to check your GCSE syllabus to find out which other shopping items your students will need to know.

In addition, students will need to be able to:

- ask where particular shops are.
  La boucherie, s'il vous plaît?

- ask about and understand opening times.
  Le supermarché ouvre/ferme à quelle heure?

- ask and understand about non-availability.
  Avez-vous. . .?
  Non, nous n'avons pas/plus de. . .

A popular GCSE question links shops with the items they sell. Practise this with your students for each shop. Draw on an OHT an empty frame with the shop name in French at the top of the frame. Write shopping items on separate pieces of acetate. A student comes to the OHP and places the correct items in a selected shop. Time the activity and challenge another student to beat the record set by the first student.

Extend the activity by asking students to write a list of as many items as possible in a given time for named shops, e.g.

Qu'est-ce qu'on peut acheter dans une pharmacie (un supermarché)?

On the right-hand side of the board, write shopping items in a jumbled order. On the left-hand side of the board write a list of shops. Students take it in turns to come to the board and draw an arrow from the item to the appropriate shop.

Further practice on this topic can be found in **Vital 2**, *Unité 5*.

USE OF ASSESSMENT WORKSHEETS

Worksheet 79

If the student's drawing is not clear, ask him/her to label it in English to check comprehension.

1
– Bonjour, monsieur. Vous désirez?
– Je voudrais une baguette, s'il vous plaît.
– Une baguette. Et avec ça?
– Je voudrais aussi une bouteille d'eau minérale.
– Oui, monsieur. Et avec ça?
– Quatre bananes et des oranges.
– Oui, monsieur. C'est tout?
– Oui. Ça fait combien?
– Ça fait 90 francs, monsieur.
– 90 francs. Merci. Au revoir, monsieur.
– Au revoir.

2
– Bonjour, madame. Vous désirez?
– Je voudrais trois pommes.
– Trois pommes. Oui, madame.
– Et deux pêches.

– Deux pêches. . . et avec ça?
– Je voudrais aussi une bouteille de coca-cola.
– Une bouteille de coca-cola. C'est tout?
– Non, 200g de fromage et un paquet de chips, s'il vous plaît.
– 200g de fromage et un paquet de chips. Voilà, madame. C'est tout?
– Oui, c'est tout. Ça fait combien?
– Ça fait 63 francs, madame.
– Merci. Au revoir, madame.
– Au revoir, madame.

Worksheet 80

– Regardez les pêches! Seulement 10 francs le kilo! 10 francs le kilo!
– Premières poires de l'été! Les poires à seulement 9 francs le kilo! 9 francs le kilo!
– Tomates de la région! 8 francs le kilo! 8 francs le kilo!
– Goûtez les pommes! 11 francs le kilo! Sensass! Un kilo de pommes pour 11 francs!
– Fromage du berger! Seulement 7 francs, les deux cents grammes! Seulement 7 francs, le fromage!
– Une grande bouteille de coca-cola ne coûte aujourd'hui que 10 francs! Oui, 10 francs la grande bouteille!
Orangina! Une petite bouteille d'orangina! Aujourd'hui à prix réduit! 6 francs! Seulement 6 francs la bouteille!
– Biscuits au chocolat! Un paquet, 8 francs! 8 francs pour le paquet de biscuits au chocolat! C'est fantastique!

Worksheet 81

1
– Bonjour, monsieur. Vous désirez?
– Je voudrais deux paquets de biscuits, s'il vous plaît.
– Deux paquets de biscuits. Et avec ça?
– Deux bouteilles d'eau minérale.
– Deux bouteilles d'eau minérale. C'est tout?

– Non, je voudrais aussi deux cents grammes de fromage et quatre tranches de jambon.
– Deux cents grammes de fromage et quatre tranches de jambon. Oui, monsieur. Et avec ça?
– Je voudrais aussi six bananes, s'il vous plaît.
– Six bananes. Oui, monsieur. C'est tout?
– Oui. Ça fait combien?
– Ça fait 80 francs, monsieur.
– 80 francs. Merci. Au revoir, madame.
– Au revoir.

2
– Bonjour, madame. Vous désirez?
– Je voudrais 200g de fromage, s'il vous plaît.
– 200g de fromage. Oui, madame.
– Et quatre poires.
– Oui. Quatre poires. . . et avec ça?
– Je voudrais aussi un kilo de tomates.
– Un kilo de tomates. C'est tout?
– Non, deux paquets de chips et une bouteille d'eau minérale, s'il vous plaît.
– Deux paquets de chips et une bouteille d'eau minérale. Voilà, madame. C'est tout?
– Oui, c'est tout. Ça fait combien?
– Ça fait 48 francs, madame.
– Merci. Au revoir, monsieur.
– Au revoir, madame.

Worksheet 82

To check that students understand the symbols, practise the dialogues in class before students work in pairs.

Worksheets 85 and 86

Students must write at least three items on their shopping lists. To achieve the outcome the items must include weights, volumes or containers, as appropriate.

ANSWERS FOR ASSESSMENT WORKSHEETS

Worksheet 79
1A.
2 3 apples, 2 peaches, bottle of coca cola, 200 grams of cheese, packet of crisps.

Worksheet 80
peaches 10F, pears 9F, tomatoes 8F, apples 11F, cheese 7F, coca cola 10F, orangina 6F, chocolate biscuits 8F.

Worksheet 81
1 Paul buys: biscuits, mineral water, cheese, ham, bananas.
2 Nicole buys: 200 grams of cheese, 4 pears, kilo of tomatoes, 2 bags of crisps, a bottle of mineral water.

Worksheet 84
a 2; b peaches, pears, apples; c mineral water; d bottle; e 300 grams; f cheese; g biscuits and crisps; h apples.

Au téléphone

Objectives

- to ask to speak to someone on the telephone, stating and spelling your name.
- to identify the caller's name.
- to understand a simple written telephone message.

TEACHING NOTES

STUDENT'S BOOK, page 75

Introduce this unit by emphasising the importance of a 'telephone manner' in the modern day working world. It is by no means unusual for a British firm to have telephone and fax connections with European partners and associates. Ask students how they would react on work experience if someone called from France. Explain that being able to handle the situation by knowing the right expressions is a great confidence booster. Also, if you are in France and want to call home to the UK, it is useful to know beforehand what to do.

Discuss the importance of being able to use the telephone and ask students to think of situations where they may need to do so.

Learning the French alphabet is relatively easy whilst being very useful. Explain that there are often situations where, because you are a foreigner, you will need to spell out your name or ask for unfamiliar words to be spelt.

Ask the students to look at the photographs. Ask if they have ever used a phone card.

What are the advantages of a card over coins? Did they know that they can use a BT Chargecard in France?

Background information

The French are justifiably proud of their modern telecommunications system. Many people have a 'Minitel' and via the telephone system, they can access banks or buy rail or cinema tickets. The Internet (*le service*) is popular in France.

Phone cards are used far more often than coins and can be bought from *tabacs*.

Explain to students that all telephone numbers in France have recently been prefixed with two digits; all telephone numbers are now ten digits.

STUDENT'S BOOK, pages 76–77
Objective 1: to ask to speak to someone on the telephone

Presenting the language

Remind the students that they had to learn the alphabet in English in nursery and their first years at school. The use of song to teach the alphabet is popular because it divides letters into groups, remembered more readily if they rhyme. Tell them that this is how French

children must have learned their letters: ABC DEFG HIJ KLM NOP QRS TUV WX Y et Z.

Ask students which letters they think sound like the English letters. List those in one colour. Concentrate on the remaining letters. Which sound similar except for the vowel sound and which ones are totally different?

Activity 1

a & b

– a b c d e f g h i j k l m n o p q r s t u v w x y z

After the students have listened and repeated the sounds, they could make a class recording. Play the tape again, pausing at each letter so the sound is fresh and they record immediately after listening.

Ask a student to come to the board. With a ruler, this student plays the role of teacher or conductor and as he or she points to the letters, the whole class must recite.

Differentiation   Some students may need extra practice. It will help to link a sound with a picture, for example 'B Watch' or a dentist 'say A'. The more the students invent themselves, the more they are likely to remember.

Activity 2

Explain that in Canada everyone has their own personalised number plate. The number on the car refers to the driver's licence rather than the car. When you buy a new car in Canada, you affix your own number plate to it.

a, b & c

– 45L QYZ
– GHA A76
– P1O K1N

After completing the exercises, let the students design their own number plates. Place them on the table at the front. A student volunteers to be a traffic warden and reads aloud the plate he or she has decided to give a parking ticket to.

Activity 3

The answers have been recorded on tape.

– Jean Paul Gaultier: Jean: J-E-A-N; Paul: P-A-U-L; Gaultier: G-A-U-L-T-I-E-R.
– Jean Alesi: Jean: J-E-A-N; Alesi: A-L-E-S-I.
– Antoine de Caunes: Antoine: A-N-T-O-I-N-E; de: D-E; Caunes: C-A-U-N-E-S.
– Gérard Depardieu: Gérard: G-E-R-A-R-D; Depardieu: D-E-P-A-R-D-I-E-U.

Ask if they can think of any more French speakers (e.g. Celine Dion, Jacques Villeneuve, Philippe Albert, etc.).

Differentiation   For those who need further practice, spell in French the names of some famous pop groups (e.g. Blur, Oasis, 3T, Backstreet Boys, etc.) or some famous cars

(e.g. Citroen, BMW, etc.). More able students could practise spelling their own names and home towns, as if registering in a hotel in France.

Activity 4

Practise *Je voudrais parler à. . .* as a global expression, said so many times it will come easily. Point to students at random and say, for example, *Je voudrais parler à Donna.*

Practise *C'est qui?*, using photos of famous personalities. Ask the class *C'est qui?* and elicit answers, e.g. *C'est Princess Diana*. Eventually students take turns asking the question.

– Bonjour, je voudrais parler à Monsieur Lebrun, s'il vous plaît.
– C'est de la part de qui?
– Je m'appelle Madame Brown, B-R-O-W-N.

Activity 5

a & b

– Bonjour, je voudrais parler à Madame Vernon, s'il vous plaît.
– C'est de la part de qui?
– Je m'appelle Monsieur Leclerc, L-E-C-L-E-R-C.

Differentiation   When more able students have worked the dialogue successfully, ask questions of them orally, e.g. *Dialogue A – elle voudrait parler à Madame Leblanc?/Dialogue B – c'est qui?*, etc.

Students could pretend to be secretaries. The teacher spells out names for them to write down.

'Hangman' is called *le pendu* in French and is useful for teaching spelling.

Activity 6

Less able students may need extra help with this. If so, work through on the board/OHP with them the words that they would have to change to make a new dialogue.

Differentiation   More able students will finish this exercise fairly quickly. You could allow them to extend their dialogues to include one more exchange:

– Je vous passe Monsieur Leblanc
– Merci. Au revoir.

Although they will not be assessed on this extra language, it can sometimes be very motivating for students to go beyond what is on the page.

Patterns of language

Point out that the expression *je voudrais* is being used again, this time to say 'I would like (to speak to. . .)'. Remind students how useful this expression is and elicit uses for it (e.g. ordering in a café, shopping for clothes/food, etc.). Explain that the conditional tense is used because it would be considered impolite to use the present tense 'I want to speak to. . .'.

STUDENT'S BOOK, page 78
Objective 2: to identify the caller's name

Presenting the language

Some students may find telephone dialogues easier to follow if the teacher uses pictures, or with the help of two people to present this language. The less able may also need prompting. If so, write the dialogues on the board or OHP in different colours for the two speakers.

Activity 1
b
– Bonjour, je voudrais parler à Madame Smith, s'il vous plaît.
– C'est de la part de qui?
– C'est Madame Laroche.
– Comment ça s'écrit?
– L-A-R-O-C-H-E.

Activity 2
1 Bonjour, je voudrais parler à Madame Green, s'il vous plaît.
2 Bonjour, je voudrais parler à Monsieur Smith, s'il vous plaît.
3 Bonjour, je voudrais parler à Madame Thomas, s'il vous plaît.
4 Bonjour, je voudrais parler à Madame Vernon, s'il vous plaît.

Activity 3
It was to the annoyance of their UK fans that Eric Cantona and David Ginola were not chosen to play for France in Euro 96. This exercise exploits that situation!

Differentiation   More able students could make up further dialogues or be challenged to write out their three dialogues within a certain time. Less able students who find too much writing demotivating, could make a photo story out of one dialogue only by finding photos of the stars from football magazines and adding speech bubbles to them.

Patterns of language

Explain that the expressions *C'est qui?* and *C'est de la part de qui?* are both used to ask who is calling. Point out that while it is easier to use the shorter version, it is obviously important to be able to recognise the longer expression. *C'est qui?* might be used in an informal situation amongst friends, but the unit concentrates on the use of *C'est de la part de qui?* which is more polite and businesslike.

STUDENT'S BOOK, page 79
Objective 3: to understand a simple written telephone message

Presenting the language

Only the hours and half hours are taught in this unit. Revise or introduce the numbers 1–30 (see Teacher's Book, unit 1, for ideas for presenting the numbers). Explain that the 24-hour clock is used more often for appointments and elicit reasons for this. Explain that the small 'h' means *heure* and that telling the time in French is easier than they probably think.

Have flashcards of places the students already know or can guess (e.g. *la discothèque, le cinéma, le restaurant, l'hôtel*, etc.). Have some more flashcards with some times in the evening on them. Put the places on the board, then choose two students' names and say *Michelle et Peter, rendezvous à la discothèque à 20h.* Put the time card next to the disco card. Repeat this a few times with other place and time cards or until students really understand the exercise. Ask students to repeat the rendezvous arrangements after you and move on, so that eventually a volunteer matches the cards.

Activity 1

For part **a** of the activity, read through the six messages and check the students' understanding before completing the matching activity.

For part **b**, remind students that answering questions such as these in English, is the type of exercise they would meet at basic level GCSE.

Differentiation   For those who need further practice, make three piles of smaller cards and play 'The time, the place' in groups. The third pile has the names of either students in the

group or famous people. Shuffle the cards and see if the students can make sentences such as *Andrew et Kylie, rendezvous à la disco à 20h.*

Meanwhile, more able students who complete the comprehension exercise quickly, could make up three further comprehension questions for their partner. Very able students could even be asked the questions in French.

Patterns of language

Point out that *à la/au* is used to say 'to the' according to the gender of the place, and explain that *au* is simply used to replace *à le.*

It could be pointed out to more able students that *a telephoné* is the past tense.

TRANSITION TO GCSE

This unit covers most of the requirements for GCSE. In addition, students must be able to understand and give a telephone number. As numbers often cause problems, considerable practice is required at regular intervals.

For example, write a dozen telephone numbers in figures on the board. One student comes to

the front, you say one of the telephone numbers and the student rubs that number off the board. Make it a race to see if the class can rub out all the numbers before the lesson ends.

Further practice on this topic can be found in **Vital 1**, *Unité 10.*

USE OF ASSESSMENT WORKSHEETS

Worksheet 89

In activity 2, the names are spelt on the recording.

NB Writing is not assessed in the outcomes for this unit.

1

Dialogue 1

– Allô. Ici la compagnie Shell.
– Bonjour, madame. Je voudrais parler à Monsieur Brown, s'il vous plaît.
– Monsieur Brown n'est pas dans son bureau en ce moment. Il peut vous rappeler à 11h?
– Oui.
– C'est de la part de qui?
– C'est Monsieur Leclerc.
– Leclerc. Ça s'écrit comment, s'il vous plaît?

– L-E-C-L-E-R-C.
– Bon, merci. Au revoir.
– Au revoir

Dialogue 2

– Allô. Ici la compagnie Shell.
– Bonjour, madame. Je voudrais parler à Monsieur Brown, s'il vous plaît.
– Monsieur Brown n'est pas dans son bureau en ce moment. Il peut vous rappeler à 11h?
– Oui.
– C'est de la part de qui?
– C'est Monsieur Alexandre.
– Alexandre. Ça s'écrit comment, s'il vous plaît?
– A-L-E-X-A-N-D-R-E.
– Bon, merci. Au revoir.
– Au revoir

Dialogue 3
– Allô. Ici la compagnie Shell.
– Bonjour, madame. Je voudrais parler à Monsieur Brown, s'il vous plaît.
– Monsieur Brown n'est pas dans son bureau en ce moment. Il peut vous rappeler à 11h?
– Oui.
– C'est de la part de qui?
– C'est Monsieur Lebrun.
– Lebrun. Ça s'écrit comment, s'il vous plaît?
– L-E-B-R-U-N.
– Bon, merci. Au revoir.
– Au revoir

Dialogue 4
– Allô. Ici la compagnie Shell.
– Bonjour, madame. Je voudrais parler à Monsieur Brown, s'il vous plaît.
– Monsieur Brown n'est pas dans son bureau en ce moment. Il peut vous rappeler à 11h?
– Oui.
– C'est de la part de qui?
– C'est Monsieur Vervier.
– Vervier. Ça s'écrit comment, s'il vous plaît?
– V-E-R-V-I-E-R.
– Bon, merci. Au revoir.
– Au revoir.

2
a
– Allô. Ici la compagnie Shell.
– Bonjour, monsieur. Je voudrais parler à Monsieur Brown, s'il vous plaît.
– Monsieur Brown n'est pas dans son bureau en ce moment. Il peut vous rappeler cet après-midi.
– Oui.
– C'est de la part de qui?
– C'est Madame Coltier.
– Coltier. Ça s'écrit comment, s'il vous plaît?
– C-O-L-T-I-E-R.
– Bon, merci. Au revoir.
– Au revoir

b
– Allô. Ici la compagnie Shell.
– Bonjour, monsieur. Je voudrais parler à Monsieur Brown, s'il vous plaît.
– Monsieur Brown n'est pas dans son bureau en ce moment. Il peut vous rappeler cet après-midi.
– Oui.
– C'est de la part de qui?
– C'est Madame Gagnon.
– Gagnon. Ça s'écrit comment, s'il vous plaît?
– G-A-G-N-O-N.
– Bon, merci. Au revoir.
– Au revoir

c
– Allô. Ici la compagnie Shell.
– Bonjour, monsieur. Je voudrais parler à Monsieur Brown, s'il vous plaît.
– Monsieur Brown n'est pas dans son bureau en ce moment. Il peut vous rappeler cet après-midi.
– Oui.
– C'est de la part de qui?
– C'est Madame Thomas.
– Thomas. Ça s'écrit comment, s'il vous plaît?
– T-H-O-M-A-S.
– Bon, merci. Au revoir.
– Au revoir

d
– Allô. Ici la compagnie Shell.
– Bonjour, monsieur. Je voudrais parler à Monsieur Brown, s'il vous plaît.
– Monsieur Brown n'est pas dans son bureau en ce moment. Il peut vous rappeler cet après-midi.
– Oui.
– C'est de la part de qui?
– C'est Madame Laroche.
– Laroche. Ça s'écrit comment, s'il vous plaît?
– L-A-R-O-C-H-E.
– Bon, merci. Au revoir.
– Au revoir

ANSWERS FOR ASSESSMENT WORKSHEETS

Worksheet 89
1 a3, b4, c2, d1.
2 Mme. Coltier, Mme. Gagnon, Mme. Thomas, Mme. Laroche.

Worksheet 90
a3, b2, c1, d4.

Worksheet 91
a at the cinema; b M. Leblanc; c M. Mazarand; d Mme. Raymond; e 3 p.m.; f 10 p.m.; g sports centre; h Jean-Paul.